KINGDOM CURRENCY

VOLUME THREE

FOR STUDENTS, GRADUATES AND BUSINESS MEN

How to Achieve Excellence, Get the Best Jobs Without Application and Build a Global Business Brand.

Iredafenevesho **OWOLABI**

Copyright © Iredafenevesho Owolabi 2018

All rights reserved. No part of this publication may be reproduced, stored in a retrieval system, or transmitted in any form or by any means, electronic, mechanical, photocopying, recording, or otherwise, without the prior written permission of the author.

Unless otherwise stated, scripture quotations are from **HOLY BIBLE, KING JAMES VERSION** ®. KJV ®. Copyright © 1982 by Thomas Nelson. Used by permission. All rights reserved.

Iredafenevesho **OWOLABI**

KEYS FOR BIBLE TRANSLATIONS USED:
AMP - The Amplified Bible,
ESV – English Standard Version,
GWT – God's Word Translation,
MSG - The Message Translation,
NASB – New American Standard Bible,
NIV - New International Version,
NKJV - New King James Version,
NLT - New Living Translation,
TLB - The Living Bible.

ISBN
Paper back: 9781987677881

Quantity Sales: Special discounts available on quantity purchases by corporations, associations, churches, bookstores, wholesalers and others. Place your orders directly via. Tel: (+234) 8187960599.

Orders for college textbooks/course adoption use: Also contact via Tel (+234) 8187960599.

The revelations herein are expressed from the author's perspective and spiritual insight on the subject matter covered. It is published with the understanding that the writer is not rendering legal, medical, financial or other professional service. If legal advice or other expert assistance is required, the services of a competent professional should be sought. The author and publisher are in no way liable for any misuse of the material.

ACKNOWLEDGEMENTS

All the glory belongs to God who has caused me to be a blessing to the billions of people who would benefit from the principles in this book.

I want to use this medium to also tender my unreserved gratitude to my ever beautiful wife, Pharm. Dr. Precious Owolabi. You are an epitome of love, praise and virtue. Thank you for your encouragement on this particular project.

I want to thank my Parents, Elder Laifotape Owolabi and Pastor (Mrs.) Justina Ruth Owolabi for being a pillar of strength and an avalanche of love to me.

I acknowledge my Parents-in-law, Pastor Sam Kikeme and (Mrs.) Mary Kikeme, thank you for your faith in my visions.

To a great mentor and father, Pastor (Dr.) Sam Adodo, I appreciate your diligent contributions to this book. You are a sage by every standard.

To Wisdom Aigbose, thanks for the creativity and dexterity you displayed on the cover design. I also acknowledge PD (Mr.) and (Mrs.) Ademola and Christiana Usuanlele for being a part of this project. God bless you all greatly.

TABLE OF CONTENT
ACKNOWLEDGEMENT   v

INTRODUCTION   001-018
Getting a Job or contract without Application:
a Myth, a Reality or a Possibility?
Who is a Student?
Who is a Graduate?
Who is a Businessman?
Employment versus deployment
What has Kingdom Currency got to do with these?

CHAPTER ONE:
THE CURRENCY OF EXCELLENCE   019-057
What is Excellence?
The Spirit of Excellence and the Excellent Spirit
Excellence as a Kingdom Currency
Getting the Best Jobs and Contracts by the Currency of Excellence
Building a Global Business Brand with the Currency of Excellence
Keys for Converting the Currency of Excellence into Tangible Wealth
Charge
Affirmations
Food for Thoughts

CHAPTER TWO:
THE CURRENCY OF VISION   058-102
What is Vision?
Purpose and Vision
The Vision Statement
The Vision and the Provision

Vision as a Kingdom Currency
Achieving Excellence by the Currency of Vision
Getting the Best Jobs and Contracts by the
Currency of Vision
Lessons from Joseph's Story
Building a Global Business Brand with the
 Currency of Vision
Keys for Converting the Currency of Vision
into Tangible Wealth
Charge
Affirmations
Food for Thoughts

CHAPTER THREE:
THE CURRENCY OF DILIGENCE   149-174
What is Diligence?
Diligence as a Kingdom Currency
Achieving Excellence by the Currency of Diligence
Getting the Best Jobs by the Currency of Diligence
Building a Global Business Brand with
the Currency of Diligence
Keys for Converting the Currency of Diligence
into Tangible Wealth
Charge
Affirmations
Food for Thoughts

CHAPTER FOUR:
THE CURRENCY OF CHARACTER   149-174
What is Character?
Branding and Character
Branding and Packaging
Achieving Excellence by the Currency
of Character

Getting the Best Jobs by the Currency of Character
Building a Global Business Brand with the
Currency of Character
Keys for Converting the Currency of Character
into Tangible Wealth
Charge
Affirmations
Food for Thoughts

CHAPTER FIVE:
THE CURRENCY OF A GOOD NETWORK 175-193
What is Network?
Getting the Best Jobs by the Currency of a
 Good Network
Building a Global Business Brand with the
Currency of a Good Network
Keys for Converting the Currency of a Good
Network into Tangible Wealth
Charge
Affirmations
Food for Thoughts

NOTES: 194-197

INTRODUCTION
Getting a Job or contract without Application: a Myth, a Reality or a Possibility?

It was about 12:30pm one sunny Saturday, when I sat down with my eyes ajar and mouth salivating. I was hearing some of the most compelling stories I had ever heard coming live from a man I always admired from a distance. It was in a meeting with a captain of industry based in Abuja, the Federal Capital of Nigeria. This man had explored the lengths, breadths and heights of a great career before he ventured into running two private firms with an annual turnover of 9 figures and a net worth that ran into 10 figures. He began to share some of his personal experiences of how he had experienced an unusual dimension of dominion by which he got the best jobs in those days. He shared remarkable testimonies regarding how he had worked in 6 different reputable banks in big Nigerian cities like Port Harcourt, Lagos and Abuja. Interestingly, he worked in these places as a top notch manager. He mentioned some of his striking life stories and experiences with these banks. He spoke of how he never wrote an application for these jobs, but yet got the best jobs in his career days. He said he would have got these top notch jobs and begun working for six months before the management would tell him that his file was empty. They would then inform him that they needed some of his documents for documentation purposes. That is when they would request him to bring his documents just to fulfill all righteousness. Wow! This is amazing. After 6 months of having worked and received salaries? Who does that? Mind you, all of these encounters hardly had anything to do with his certificate or college grades. He simply was operating with Kingdom Currency without really knowing it.

After that meeting, I was awestruck that 6 different reputable banks with high profile employment processes and requirements would employ this man in his career days without an application. One would have thought he did it through some sharp practices but that does not happen with 1, 2, 3... and continue to recur until he gets into the top ranks in 6 different reputable banks. There had to be some time tested principle which that man had engaged in his phenomenal experience through his career path. Reason being that he did not only get employed without applications but rose to the top of the cadre in several of these different establishments. As he told his story, it was obvious that this was no gimmick and that he achieved all that without lobbying or engaging in corrupt affiliations and connections. I had heard about miracles before, but this time I was watching one unveil right in front of me. I never knew why God made this man share that story but it was not too long before it became clear. After that meeting, I kept wondering about that man's testimony. It stayed on my mind for so long until the Lord began to speak to me concerning that man's personal story.

God told me that this was His desire for every kingdom citizen. He said to me, "No kingdom citizen was ever meant to be unemployed regardless of the rate of unemployment in any particular nation where he resides and despite the economic situation on earth". He also made it clear to me that the best jobs ought to chase after kingdom citizens and not the other way round. He gave me this illustration: if the son of a well known reputable king wanted a job, would he need to struggle to get one? If you were the son of a governor or a president and you needed a job, what would it be like? God then asked me, "Would you need to go through the hassles which lots of Nigerian graduates suffer in order to get one? Or would you manage a meager salary at an odd job for lack of a better one?" By reason of being the son or daughter of royalty, such a person would not lack the best opportunities required to satisfy his desire for a job. It would be a case of selecting from several different available juicy options rather than a fruitless search from one firm to another. It would not be a random endeavor but a precise and definite appointment with little or no formality involved. As far as I was concerned, God was correct. He went on to say to me, "If sons and daughters of earthly governors, presidents and kings can have the best jobs around the world without any struggle, how much easier would it be for the son of the King of kings to get one?" It then dawned on me that if our Heavenly Father was truly the Governor among the nation (and He is), Kingdom Citizens have no business with unemployment and underemployment. It was then God began to show me the secrets to that dimension and asked me to coach others in that area. He then instructed me to put it down in writing in form of a book. That was how I got inspired to write this very book in your hands now. God mandated me to write a book that would cut down unemployment and underemployment by seventy five percent and increase business creation and investments by eighty percent.

Do you want a high paying job to start your journey into career? Or you just want to transfer to a bigger, better and more reputable organization? Do you want to build a global business brand that would affect the nations of the earth right from where you are? Maybe you just want to achieve personal excellence in your life and need some more divine energy to propel you on that journey. If you fall into any of such categories or a similar one, then this is your day. Right in your hand is that book that would ensure your big break in gaining personal excellence and help you get the best jobs or contracts without the hassles that many go through. This is that one book that would enable you build the globally relevant business brand you have always dreamed about. By the principles in this volume, you will get the blueprint that would catapult you into the reality of having all your desires, goals and aspirations adequately met.

Since I believe that not everyone is called to become a mega business man, this book is also tailored for those who are not cut out for running their own businesses. After all, if everyone ran his own personal enterprise without taking a job in another man's business establishment, who would be in the offices and organizations making the system work? I believe there is a place for everyone and it could be in business, in career, in academics, etc. The purpose of this book therefore, is not to exalt one particular field, profession or path over the other. Rather this book would act as a guide to lead you and inspire you on whichever path God has ordained for you, or that you have chosen to take in your journey through life. Perhaps you are not so sure what path to take with regards to academics, career, business, profession or life in general; as you read this book you would receive absolute clarity. I am pretty sure this is not the kind of book you would want to start reading and stop midway without completing and going over it for several times. I am certain of that because, no matter who you are, where you are from, what you do or where you are headed in life, you will fall into one category or more of the three categories to which this book is addressed. It is either you are a student, a graduate or a businessperson. Now this statement may surprise you a little bit, probably because you have never given that a thought. But it is true! To verify that, maybe we need to understand who a student, a graduate or a businessman is respectively.

Who is a Student?

The term "student" is usually used to refer to anyone attending a school to gain knowledge and education or anyone studying a course and learning in an academic institution. On a general scale, the word "student" also comes to mind when speaking about learning outside a formal educational institution. It can be used to describe someone who is learning on a particular topic through self education. It is also used in a different perspective to refer to someone who understudies an expert in a particular field by studying his works or by being a follower of him. A disciple for example, could also be referred to as a student of his master, depending on the context in which the word is used. Most times when the word "student" is heard, what comes to the mind of some people is a young child, teenager or youth going to school on a uniform with a backpack. In some parts of society it looks strange to associate the word student with adults who are not necessarily on a post graduate academic course of study. But in the broadest sense of the word, *a student is anyone seeking to learn or to grow by gaining knowledge and, or experience, whether in a formal educational system or outside one.*

It hardly ever occurs to most folks that everyone is a student as long as he applies his heart and mind to learning something. There is never an end to knowledge and therefore there is no end to learning or to being a student. Albert Einstein made a very profound statement when he said "Once you stop learning, you start dying." How true! As long as you still have life, you are a student of life. You are constantly learning something new no matter how little it may seem because we learn every day. It is only a matter of what value or benefits the knowledge or experience we have acquired offers. If we learn every day, why then do many people seem not to be advancing in life? It is unfortunate that though we learn every day, many times we are not conscious of the things we have learned. Hence we never do anything with what we have learned from life's experience or from formal institutions. It is what you do with the knowledge you have that differentiates you from another; not how much of knowledge you have acquired.

Many students are faced with serious challenges such that most times only a few of them ever overcome. One of such challenges they face is that of achieving excellence. Some others have a fear for tomorrow not knowing what the future in their given line of study holds for them. While many of them also, have been made to pursue careers that they are not suited for because of the perceived high prospects of gaining employment with an academic degree in that field. There is a typical example of a man I admire who shared his experience in a book he titled, "What I would do differently". This man has become so successful in his life as a Pastor and as a leading Success Coach in Nigeria. He wrote this book to share with his readers some of the mistakes he made on his journey through life. This was done in a bid to help others learn from his experiences and to make them avoid the same mistakes he made while on his success journey. His name is Sam Adeyemi, the President of Success Power International and Pastor of Daystar Christian Center. In this book, he spoke about how he was made to study Civil Engineering because his parents wanted him to and not really because that was his passion or desire. His father was a building contractor and wanted him to work with him after school. His father, like several other well meaning parents, had intended for him to join him in his business and eventually get to the point of taking it over. While Sam Adeyemi was in his second year in college, his father had already registered a company and made him a director in the company. His fortune seemed to have already been decided by his parents who had good plans for him.

It turned out that by the time Sam Adeyemi was done with school, there was no business in his father's establishment anymore. Since his father's business had crashed, he had no choice but to go out on a job search. It took him 20 months after he graduated from school and completed the mandatory Youth Service in Nigeria to get a job in a construction company. One day as he was working as a site engineer on a multi million naira project, his director lashed out at him and criticized him. He felt so sorry for himself and lost his mood. He began to blame his dad. He lamented and said to himself "If not that my dad's business did not work out, what business did I have searching for a job somewhere?" He shed tears and felt very bad about his situation. Thank God that Sam at this time had begun to develop a personal relationship with God. When he went back to his site office in his moody state, he heard God console him. God encouraged him and told him not to worry about his situation because He had greater plans for him. He already had a personal relationship with the King of the kingdom of heaven and hence God helped him come out of that frustration by giving him a vision for a brighter and a better future far removed from what his mind could ever imagine. God made him understand that He had beautiful plans for his life and was destined to promote and bless him.

Many students are on this same path, heading in a similar direction where they have chosen to study a particular discipline that they did not really want due to one circumstance or the other. In some cases, it is a result of peer pressure and societal expectations. But in other cases, it is engineered by parents who are still trying to influence their children's career choice and ultimately their destiny without knowing the implications. They forget that God has a plan for every child and must be carefully sought as we raise our children and guide them through school. As parents, we must be careful not to overly try to run our children's lives by dictating to them what path to take in business or career. As parents we can make suggestions to our children on what path they should consider. As we make suggestions, we must allow them be the ones to pilot the decision making process through the guidance of the Holy Spirit as co-pilot.

This book would not only help student readers to achieve excellence in their academics. It would also teach them how to chart their course in career and business after their various academic programs while avoiding the confusion that follow most students after graduation. It would act as a guide, showing each student what they require to make the most of their destiny on earth. For those who are not necessarily students in an academic institution, who probably are students of life, this book would help you achieve excellence and gain mastery of your personal life. Every student is a potential master and ought to understand that learning is a lifelong process. It is not regimented to the four walls of a formal educational system. So whether you are in a formal educational program or not, you should consider this book to be of benefit to you. This is because what makes a student is the learning process and all other formalities are secondary.

Who is a Graduate?

A graduate simply refers to someone who has completed the requirement of an academic degree. Graduates are supposed to be assets to every nation where they find themselves. They are supposed to add value to the society the moment they leave the school systems where they were trained. While some graduates have begun to add value to their society, a large number have become a liability to the society. There are millions of graduates who have left school not knowing what direction to take in life. Some climb up the ladder of a career discipline and arrive at the pinnacle of that career just to discover they do not have any business going in that direction in the first place.

According to Sam Adeyemi's story, part of which was earlier narrated above, he came to a point where he felt that he had made a costly mistake working in that construction company. He began to wonder what he was even doing on that site in the first place. It would also interest you to know that out of frustration, Sam Adeyemi once planned to get out of Nigeria and be gone for good as a graduate. This is the honest plight of the average graduate in most third world nations today. But by God's divine arrangement, all his plans did not work out. He therefore accepted God's verdict and went on to build a global success coaching empire and a mega church. Sam Adeyemi has been able to successfully establish himself as a brand in the speaking industry of Nigeria, a feat only few people in the country have achieved. This man now commands a wide influence cutting across different categories of people around the world. He now adds value to millions of lives globally because he was able to discover his value. What if he had escaped the hardship of his country without discovering himself as a graduate? The lives that have been impacted by him around the world would probably have been left groping in the dark path of frustration. Had he travelled out of the country also, he would have been like the man who was sitting on acres of diamonds but sold his piece of property in search of fortune elsewhere not knowing that he was sitting on a diamond mine the whole time. This is the predicament of many graduates in the underdeveloped society today. They graduate and begin to seek a route of escape from their countries because they are in search of greener pastures elsewhere. There is absolutely nothing wrong with migrating to another nation if God is leading you in that direction. Even at that, you must go there with a mentality that you are the one that would add value to them and not the other way round no matter the sophistication of that nation you want to migrate to.

Most graduates forget that they were schooled to become people who would be able to add value to the society. As a graduate, the expectation is that value must be added to the society through you, no matter where you find yourself. Always think in terms of what value you can add to the place rather than always looking for what value you can get from that place. This is because wealth only gravitates to those who add value to their environment. Money itself is known as a medium of exchange, a store of value and a measure of value, it is only exchanged in return for value. **That means, the more value you add to a system the more money you would attract from that system in exchange for value.** Because Sam Adeyemi was able to discover himself after he graduated from school and had experienced some serious setbacks in life, he was able to add value to his immediate environment and that boosted his worth. Today he travels around the world to add value to people across different races, cultures and nations and gets paid handsomely doing that. This has become possible for him because he did not run out of his country in search of greener pastures as he earlier intended. This book is going to show you how to make the most of your life as a graduate in any nation of the world. This is not to say that you have to become a public speaker to add value but rather you have to discover your purpose in order to add value to your world. It does not matter your discipline or the grade you have graduated from school with, if you can identify your areas of passion and competence, you are good to go.

Many graduates are still frustrated because they came out of school with poor grades. They compare themselves with the first class students and measure their value based on their cumulative grade points. What a mistake! Whether you came out top of the class or average, you have something of value to offer and if you can identify this and be bold about it, there is no job that would be beyond your reach and there is no business you would venture into that would fail to blossom. Some graduates believe that they may never become great because they did poorly in school. But that is not always the case as some of the greatest inventors and richest men in history were even dropouts. Whether you are a dropout, a low grade student or a first class student, it makes no difference if you discover your value and make a commitment to serve the world with your worth. This book in your hands would show you how to harness your value in such a way that would attract the best jobs and contracts your way.

Who is a Businessman?
The word "businessman" is one that many people use in everyday communication but do not really understand its meaning. Most people confuse a businessman for an entrepreneur and vice versa. While the words businessman

and entrepreneur have a lot of similarities, they are not exactly the same thing. Why is this so? This is because the term businessman by definition is not only limited to someone who starts a business like many people have thought over the years. Rather, a businessman is a person, either male or female, who works in a commercial institution as an employee, runs an already existing business, or starts his own business enterprise. An entrepreneur on the other hand, is simply one who takes on risks by starting his own business venture and invents or introduces his own goods and services into the system. By this token, it is easy to say that an entrepreneur is a businessman, but not all businessmen are entrepreneurs. The term "entrepreneur" is a French word which is usually translated, "adventurer". While an entrepreneur is solely the person who conceives an idea and makes a business out of it, a business man could be the originator of the idea, the supplier of the raw materials needed to process the idea or a worker who assists the entrepreneur in achieving his vision. The middle men involved at all levels of distribution and marketing the entrepreneur's finished commodities to potential customers are also businessmen but they are not necessarily entrepreneurs. While an entrepreneur initiates business by creation, invention, innovation, production or manufacturing, a businessperson either initiates business or transacts business by distribution, sales, supply, marketing, and other economic activities.

According to Wikipedia, "businessmen include a founder, an owner, a manager, an executive, shareholder or an administrator in charge of total management of a corporation. But entrepreneurs are those who start and run new businesses or organizations".[1] For example, Steve Jobs and Steve Wozniak, the co-founders of the Apple Company are entrepreneurs because they initiated a business chain through their state of the art innovation of unique computers, iPods, iPads and iPhones. But those who work for the Apple Company as managers, board of directors, sales reps, distributors, marketers, suppliers, employees, including the co-founders themselves are all businessmen. Everyone who gets paid is a businessman whether you own a company, shop, supermarket or you work in one as a staff. *As long as you get paid some form of salary, allowance or you get some kind of profit in exchange for a value that you add, regardless of the venture you are involved in, you are a businessperson.* Every born again kingdom citizen who is also a bonafide member of a local church (kingdom embassy), is a businessperson whether they are involved in kingdom business or in a business whose profits are not measured in terms of souls but in monetary terms. Jesus, while He walked the streets of Jerusalem, identified Himself as a businessperson from the age of twelve. He revealed the business part of His identity one day while He was in the temple having heated conversations with the teachers there.

Now so it was that after three days they found Him in the temple, sitting in the midst of the teachers, both listening to them and asking them questions. And all who heard Him were astonished at His understanding and answers. So when they saw Him, they were amazed; and His mother said to Him, "Son, why have you done this to us? Look, your father and I have sought You anxiously. And He said to them, "Why did you seek me? DID YOU NOT KNOW THAT I MUST BE ABOUT MY FATHER'S BUSINESS?" But they did not understand the statement which He spoke to them.

Luke 2:46-50 NKJV

Jesus knew where he was deployed to at an early age and hence did not need to waste his time and energy in the wrong investment. Your business is what you intend to commit your time and life to in a bid to solve a problem profitably. Apart from monetary terms, another way to measure profitability is in terms of value added and benefit derived. Jesus' measure of profitability for His business was in the numbers of souls that were gained into the kingdom and that received of His value. Jesus faced His business squarely, giving it His complete devotion. You do not need to wait until you graduate from a tertiary institution before you begin to think about what path you are going to take towards career or business. You are better off with a clear focus either before venturing into an advanced educational pursuit or while in the process. That way you would be definite in your approach towards your education whether it is formal or informal in nature.

Employment versus Deployment
A great man, who goes by the name Dr. Myles Munroe, made a very profound statement. He said, "If you do not deploy yourself, someone else would employ you". How true! But as the world begins to advance and unemployment rates continue to skyrocket, I have noticed that another reality has begun to unfold. This unfolding reality which I have observed in the times and seasons that we are in is that "If you do not deploy yourself, no one would employ you to do what you are suited for. They would only employ you to do what you are not suited for and you would do that job with great dissatisfaction whether you are being paid well or not". Nowadays, especially in underdeveloped countries ravaged with poverty and lack of infrastructure, there are really not enough jobs to go round as little as 35 percent of the

population of job seekers. This is because for some reason, the infrastructure in such parts of the world cannot accommodate the teeming population of potential employees. In the year 2017, the National Bureau of Statistics announced that there were 4 million job losses in Nigeria between the months of January to September that year.[2] These statistics point us to the fact that the average Nigerian student and graduate needs to wake up so that they would not be victims of these sad circumstances. A failure to do this would leave the average Nigerian groping in the uncertainty and frustration that goes with being unemployed or underemployed. This book is designed with an objective to cut down unemployment by 75% and reduce the dependency ratio to the barest minimum especially in the underdeveloped and developing nations.

One day, I was heading for a training seminar in which I was scheduled to deliver the keynote when I pulled over by a newspaper vendor. That day, the newspaper I purchased carried on it a very gripping and saddening headline. The headline read "500,000 teaching jobs' portal gets 35million hits". The content of the news article gave a factual analysis of how 35 million people tried to access a portal to register for 500 slots of teaching jobs on the first night it was opened. It went further to say that 403,528 applicants were successful. And out of these successful applicants, only 500 would be given the job. As I read through the content of that publication, the need for a drastic solution became impressed upon my heart. I could hear the Spirit of God whisper to me the words "you can do something about this". The Lord then spoke to me afterwards telling me some of the root causes of the problem. He said that the reason why millions of youths and adults are wallowing in the corridors of unemployment is that they have not discovered their value. He said to me "No one was born to be employed, but to be deployed. You can only be deployed when you have been able to discover the value you add and where your value is going to be appreciated and sought for". Even though I was already familiar with the fact that no one was born to be employed but to be deployed, hearing it come from the Spirit of God this time, was as though I was being pierced by a sharp object. At this point, I was receiving a deeper revelation of that statement.

You see, in the real world, to be employed means to be used to accomplish a task and paid in return for your time and effort. Most times, this is done without you achieving your personal purpose, that is, the dreams and aspirations which you were born to explore. To be deployed on the other hand, means to be given opportunity to release your knowledge, wisdom, skill, gifting and inborn talent in order to add value in a given environment. When you have not allowed yourself to be deployed and you get yourself into any kind of employment just to get some money to pay your bills, you do not necessarily fulfill your own goals. You would remain bound by your employer to help him fulfill his own goals most times, at your expense. When you allow yourself to be deployed, you release your potential and derive fulfilment while you fulfill your own goals in the process. **Only those who deploy themselves can boast of being able to make an impact and serve out their value while they generate the resources needed to cater for their needs.** When you discover your deployment as an individual, you would immediately become free from the unemployment syndrome. This is because, the supply of employees around the world has always far surpassed the demand for them. But the supply of "deployees" is so minute compared to the demand from society for these rare species. This makes being deployed a great necessity for this present time.

What has Kingdom Currency got to do with all these?

Kingdom currencies are intangible commodities which God has provided for every kingdom citizen to take a hold of. When they take a hold of them, they would no longer be looking for jobs with very low possibility of getting the best for which they are suited. Neither would they need to struggle fruitlessly for a promotion or an appointment. Rather the best jobs, contracts, promotions and appointments would begin to look for them. This is because God has given kingdom currency to His children for them to meet their every need while on earth.

The kingdom currencies expounded on in this volume are commodities that many have taken for granted not knowing that they are even more valuable than the costliest diamond. As you begin to read this book, you would encounter five of these kingdom currencies for students, graduates and businessmen. This volume would address these currencies with respect to helping its readers achieve excellence. It would then show practical ways by which any kingdom citizen can get the best jobs and contracts without an application. As you read, it would also position you for global business success. Maybe you know someone who is still trying to find clear cut direction as a student, graduate or businessperson. It would help if you use this book as a guide to help them and also recommend it to them.

Do not read this book with a prejudice because that may shut your mind from grasping the time tested truths it presents to its readers. Read it with an open heart and allow the kingdom currencies chronicled herein to produce for you undeniable results in your career and business. Mind you, this volume can be read even without having read the previous volumes. It was designed to be a blessing regardless. But if you have studied the previous volumes, you would have a more enjoyable journey through the concepts presented in this masterpiece. Enjoy your reading!

CHAPTER ONE
THE CURRENCY OF
EXCELLENCE

"The quality of a person's life is in direct proportion to their commitment to excellence, regardless of their chosen field of endeavor."

Vince Lombardi - Athletic Coach

The world is littered with countless stories of how destinies have been destroyed by reason of blunders which have been caused by inaccuracies of workmen in different work places. I have personally heard of stories of how people lost their lives because of a doctor's error in judgment or carelessness. There are many who have taken drugs that brought them to an abrupt end in their life's journey because of wrong prescriptions that were given by a "trained doctor". Some have met their early graves due to wrong interpretation of the doctor's prescription by the Pharmacist. It is equally shocking to know that some people have undergone surgeries only to discover complications weeks after, which surfaced as a result of negligence on the part of the surgeons and nurses. They complicated the lives of people by stitching up a patient with a surgical tool forgotten inside the body of the patient after the operation. Aircrafts have taken off and crash landed in the middle of nowhere because of inaccurate maintenance done by the designated officers. Some have happened by reason of an oversight or a mistake made by the engineers or technicians in the aircraft maintenance crew during maintenance checks or just before the plane was cleared for flight. Large ships have vanished in the middle of the ocean, drowning thousands of people to death because the captain offered his second best in navigating the murky waters.

You also must have heard of buildings that collapsed and buried people alive in the ruins even before they were completed, because someone was either careless or dishonest. Mediocrity has become the order of the day in most places such that finding excellence has become an almost impossible task. Inferior materials seem to be selling faster in markets of the third world nations because people who do not mind inferiority and mediocrity prefer using cheap articles over standard materials. Hence they promote the inferior because they lack the currency of excellence and this has subjected scores of people to dangers of varying degrees.

Everywhere and every day, men of excellence are being sought for with little or no success. The world groans in pain daily due to the insecurities which humanity has subjected itself to for the lack of the currency of excellence. Right from the days of old, it has been impossible for a person known for excellence in any endeavour to go unnoticed. This is because excellence finds you out. During the reign of the Babylonian empire over Jerusalem in Bible days, the King of Babylon discovered that there was a scarcity of excellence in his entire kingdom. This caused him to send out instructions for his chief of staff to look out for excellent people in the royal family of Israel so they could be taught the language and codes that would enable them serve in the king's palace. He was specific on the caliber of people that was to be selected for the three year training. The qualities are well enumerated in the verse below.

Youths without blemish, well-favored in appearance and skillful in all wisdom, discernment, and understanding, apt in learning knowledge, competent to stand and serve in the king's palace — and to teach them the literature and language of the Chaldeans.

Dan 1:4 AMP

The king knew the value of excellence and wanted to give out strategic positions in his kingdom to people who would be able to display excellence. In his search for excellence, he sought for men who had attractive appearance, were skillful and wise, full of understanding, very teachable and quick to assimilate knowledge through learning. He also sought for competence in these people because he wanted them to serve in the best positions in his palace and kingdom. So he was very choosy and picky in his screening. Daniel had three friends who were full of the fear of God and they passed the test. They refused to defile themselves with the Babylonian recipe for excellence because they knew better. They wanted to show the world that the true recipe for excellence was not in eating the dainty meals of any palace or being nourished by food and drink from any king's table. They opted to be fed vegetables and water and in only ten days, their appearance proved to be more excellent than the others who obliged to the king's recipe for excellence in appearance (Dan 1:5-12). Daniel and his friends proved that excellence was a currency that only the King of kings can bestow in measures that far astounds the comprehension of the common minds.

And the king conversed with them, and among them all none was found like Daniel, Hananiah, Mishael, and Azariah; therefore they were assigned to stand before the king. And in all matters of wisdom and understanding concerning which the king asked them, HE FOUND THEM TEN TIMES BETTER THAN ALL THE [LEARNED] MAGICIANS AND ENCHANTERS WHO WERE IN HIS WHOLE REALM.

Dan 1:19-20 AMP

After the three year training program, it was discovered that Daniel and his three friends were no match for their colleagues in terms of excellence. They were said to be ten times far better in excellence, intelligence, wisdom and understanding compared to the others. This was because during their three year training program, they opened their minds to God for daily doses and divine impartations of excellence (Dan 1:17-18). After the training program the Bible tells us that Daniel by reason of his excellence got the best job without an application. Wow! That is amazing.

> *...so they were put on his* **REGULAR STAFF OF ADVISORS. DANIEL HELD THIS APPOINTMENT AS THE KING'S COUNSELOR** *until the first year of the reign of King Cyrus.*
>
> *Dan 1:19, 21 TLB*

If this happened for Daniel and his friends who were slaves in another kingdom, it means that anyone anywhere and at any time can get the best jobs without an application. If Daniel and the three Hebrew boys were ten times better despite denying themselves of the king's dainty meals, it means that anyone who is a kingdom citizen can achieve excellence. If Daniel and his three companions despite being captives became famous for excellence in the whole realm of Babylon and in the whole world at large, it means you can build a global business brand right from where you are. Just open your heart to receive the impartation of divine excellence as you read this highly spirited piece of writing.

What is Excellence?

Excellence is known to be a state of possessing good qualities in extraordinary measures. It is the quality that makes one outstanding in such a manner that far surpasses the normal standards. The quality of excellence is what makes a man exceptional in everything he does. Excellence is also an attribute that causes an individual to pay attention to details no matter how minute they may seem to the ordinary mind. A legendary basketball coach who was also a great basketball player spoke concerning paying attention to details. He said, "over the years I have become convinced that every detail is important and that success usually accompanies attention to little details. It is this in my judgment that makes for the difference between a champion and a near-champion".

In today's world, the word "Excellency" is used in respect and honor of dignitaries like presidents, governors, ambassadors, royalties, etc. In the kingdom of heaven, we also are royalty because we are kings and priests. We are proofs and products of the Excellency of God; hence we cannot but be excellent. The United Kingdom happens to be one of the greatest earthly kingdoms on earth today. This empire is known to be one which celebrates excellence whenever it is spotted in any individual. It recognizes them with awards which make them a part of the Most Excellent Order of the British Empire. This is a recognition granted by the British royal monarch, rewarding individuals around several nations of the world for their exceptional contributions to the arts and sciences or for their work with charitable organizations, welfare organizations, and the public service. It comprises five classes of honors known as the Grand Cross of the Most Excellent Order of the British Empire (GBE), Knight (or Dame) Commander of the Most Excellent Order Of the British Empire (KBE), Commander of the Most Excellent Order of the British Empire (CBE), Officer of the Most Excellent Order of the British Empire (OBE) and the Member of the Most Excellent Order of the British Empire (MBE). When anyone is awarded with any of these five classes of honors, such an individual becomes a member of a society of knights known as the order of chivalry or order of knighthood in the United Kingdom. This is a noble recognition that is highly respected all over the world[1]. The United Kingdom celebrates and honors excellent people because when excellence is celebrated, more excellence would show up as other people would be inspired to stand for excellence. The kingdom of heaven on the other hand, does not just expect excellence from its citizens; it codes the nature of excellence into each and every one of its citizens. That is why the Psalmist says that the children of God are the excellent ones by design in the scripture below.

AS FOR THE GODLY (THE SAINTS) WHO ARE IN THE LAND, THEY ARE THE EXCELLENT, the noble, and the glorious, IN WHOM IS ALL MY DELIGHT.
Ps 16:3 AMP

Every born again citizen of the Kingdom of heaven was recreated by God unto excellence at new birth. They are those who have been anointed with excellence. They are appointed to set forth the wonderful deeds and showcase the wonders of excellence. Since God is an excellent king who personifies the very essence of extraordinariness, He has ordained for every citizen of His kingdom to also embody His excellence. When God wants to bring about excellence in any system of society, He does it through kingdom citizens. When kingdom citizens, fail to cultivate the heavenly deposit of excellence in them, they walk in mediocrity regardless of their great capacity and high potential for excellence.

The Spirit of Excellence and the Excellent Spirit
Many years ago as a young child there was an interesting phenomenon I noticed in our interaction and playful experiments with magnets. We would play with different shapes and sizes of magnets and revel in amazement of how these magnets attracted each other when they were brought close enough. It was later on in life I understood the meaning of most of those things that appeared like a wonder to us. As I

got acquainted with science and learned about electromagnetic forces and magnetic fields, our childhood magnet play toys made more sense to me. One very notable observation we made in our interaction with magnets was, I discovered that when nails were brought into the force field of magnets, there was a force of attraction that pulled the nail toward the magnets. The more intriguing aspect of our playful observation came when we noticed that the moment we kept the nails attached to the magnet long enough, the nails after a period of time became magnetic. That is, there was a rub off of some magnetic quality on the nails such that when these magnetic nails were brought close to other nails or similar metals, they got attracted to the nail as though the magnetic nail was a magnet itself. It was later as we studied and were taught in school that I discovered that what happened to that nail was referred to as ***magnetization***. Magnetization is the process by which a substance is made temporarily or permanently magnetic by introducing it into a magnetic field. The concept of magnetization makes it easy to understand the difference between the Spirit of Excellence and the Excellent spirit.

AND IN THE GREATNESS OF YOUR EXCELLENCE You have overthrown those who rose against You; You sent forth Your wrath; It consumed them like stubble.

Ex 15:7 NKJV

Our God, who is the King of all creation, is the personification of excellence. He is the very epitome of the concept of excellence and the highest definition of the word "excellent". In fact, He is so excellent that His name is called Excellent. No wonder the Psalmist describes His name as excellent.

O LORD, OUR LORD, HOW EXCELLENT IS YOUR NAME in all the earth, Who have set Your glory above the heavens!
Ps 8:1 NKJV

He is the most Excellency and as a matter of fact is most deserving of the title "His Excellency". Many elected, selected or appointed government officials on earth today, are usually referred to as His Excellency, Her Excellency or Your Excellency. This is because in today's world, the title Excellency is used in respect and honour of dignitaries like governors, presidents, ambassadors, royalties, etc. All of these so called highly placed officials attained the positions in which they are referred to as Your Excellency either by election, selection, appointment or inheritance. But the King of all creation, the Creator that was not created, who is known as the Ancient of Days, the One who pre-existed all creation including the universe is in a class of His own as far as Excellency is concerned. He is the only Ruler that was not elected, selected, appointed, nominated nor chosen by inheritance. The heart of all the kings, presidents, ambassadors, governors are in His hands and He has the power to turn it in any direction He so pleases. He is known as the Governor among the nations, among many other titles which grant Him full authority to be addressed by the protocol, Your Excellency. Despite that, the title Your Excellency is not even befitting enough to describe God because some of His creatures have bastardized the titled with the imperfections and poor characters which they display in their so called "hallowed" offices. The Holy Spirit is the Spirit of Excellence while our recreated human spirit is the Excellent Spirit. The Excellent spirit is not something that comes automatically on a person. **Excellence in spirit is an attitude which is cultivated by virtue of the interactions we have with the Holy Spirit as kingdom species.** Just the way magnets act on nails and transmit some magnetic quality to them, the Holy Spirit performs a similar action when He is allowed to act on the human spirit. Because the Holy Spirit is the Spirit of Excellence, there is a rub off of the excellent quality of the Holy Spirit on the human spirit when we fellowship with Him, culminating in an Excellent Spirit in us. As this rub off takes place, our minds become excellent because it begins to function on the same frequency with the Spirit of Excellence.

I have heard of you, THAT THE SPIRIT OF GOD IS IN YOU, and that light and understanding and EXCELLENT WISDOM ARE FOUND IN YOU.
Dan 5:14 NKJV

Daniel was described by the king of Babylon as excellent and the king tells him why he possesses such exceptional and outstanding quality. King Belshazzar tells him that he had heard great and wonderful things about him and he was told that Daniel had the Spirit of God in him. When a man possesses the Spirit of God in him, and allows that same Spirit to rule over his mind, he begins to think excellent thoughts and that produces in him an excellent attitude. As this man maintains this excellent attitude, the man begins to produce excellent actions by reason of his excellent thoughts. When this happens, that man begins to distinguish himself everywhere he finds himself. He begins to produce new and outstanding results in whatever he does. Before long, people begin to take notice of him and in no time things begin to happen in favour of the excellent man. People begin to like him and fall in love with his unique and outstanding personality. Then doors of promotion and channels of provisions begin to open up for such a person of their own accord, without applying, bidding or lobbying for those doors to open up. This was the vital experience of Daniel by reason of the Spirit of Excellence which was within and upon him. The Bible records that Daniel was a distinguished man by reason of his excellent spirit and exceptional qualities. By reason of this, the king made plans to set him above all in his kingdom. The quality of excellence is one that cannot be hid when it is resident in an individual. It is like smoke that cannot be hid or ignored when it begins to diffuse in an environment. You cannot possess this exceptional currency known as excellence and be poor because wealth is always willingly exchanged for anything that possesses rare quality and exceptional features.

Then this DANIEL WAS DISTINGUISHED above the presidents and the satraps BECAUSE AN EXCELLENT SPIRIT was in him, and the king thought to set him over the whole realm.
Dan 6:3 AMP

Because God is the very embodiment and personification of excellence, all His works bear the mark of excellence.

Sing praises to the Lord, for He has done excellent things [gloriously]; let this be made known to all the earth.
Isa 12:5 AMP

Excellence as a Kingdom Currency
Every currency is known as such because it can be used as a medium of exchange. What makes a currency is not the fact that it is a coin with an image engraved on it or a piece of paper with some figures and a currency sign written on it. A currency is almost useless if it cannot be exchanged for something valuable or cannot be converted into a currency equivalent which is recognized and acceptable in other

states. This explains why excellence can be seen as a currency because it can be converted to money in earthly equivalents. The kingdom of heaven is a nation which has currencies. But its currencies are not coins, paper notes or cowries because it is a spiritual nation. Its currencies are intangible in nature and are convertible to currencies in earthly equivalents. Excellence is a heavenly currency which can always be converted to tangible money when it is displayed in performance and production. The cost of producing excellence is high but yet, it is nothing compared to the price for which it is demanded for in the world today. All over the world, people are more than willing to receive something of excellence in exchange for money be it naira, cedi, rand, dollar, euro or pounds.

When Michael Jordan played basketball for the Bulls, they always sold out every stadium they played in whether it was a home game or an away game. The shocking reality was that it was not the marketing skills of the stadium managers that pulled the crowds. It was the excellent display and top class performance of Michael Jordan and his teammates that always did the magic. The truth is that *your best promotional tool for marketing is your excellent service or excellent product.* When you consistently deliver excellent product and services, people would find out and when that happens, you would not be able to meet all the demands that would result. That was how Jesus, while He was on earth, always sold Himself and His ministry. He made His services to be on popular demand without engaging any marketing firm. His content was His marketing, His excellent value adding service was His typical way of promoting His brand. Every serious client would pay excellent returns and rewards for excellent performance, excellent products and excellent services. When you deliver high quality services in a very exceptional manner, people would subconsciously attune to paying more for greater satisfaction. Nobody wants to associate with a product that is of lower quality when they are faced with more excellent product or services even if it will cost them a little more. The truth remains that you would get paid average rewards for average performance and below-average rewards for below-average performance. Therefore it is up to you to choose the kind of reward you want to receive

Getting the Best Jobs and Contracts by the Currency of Excellence

- **Excellence finds you out**

The excellent one is always the favoured one. When you display excellence in anything you do, there is a great chance that you would always be considered by the decision makers when fresh opportunities are available. You would always be sought for when there is a need for someone who can do a job or contract without stress and hitches. Your name would be mentioned in critical moments even when you are absent because people always want to work with someone who can deliver excellent results. Daniel experienced a great dimension of exploits in his career. His career was characterized by uncommon feats of promotion. By virtue of his excellence, several kings either awarded contracts to him or gave him the best jobs in their cabinets during their different regimes. First it was king Nebuchadnezzar who discovered Daniel's extraordinary and exceptional qualities. When he spotted this in Daniel and his friends, he immediately granted them one of the best jobs in his kingdom.

At the end of the time set by the king to bring them in, the

chief official presented them to Nebuchadnezzar. The king talked with them, AND HE FOUND NONE EQUAL TO DANIEL, HANANIAH, MISHAEL AND AZARIAH; SO THEY ENTERED THE KING'S SERVICE. In every matter of wisdom and understanding about which the king questioned them, HE FOUND THEM TEN TIMES BETTER THAN ALL the magicians and enchanters in his whole kingdom. AND DANIEL REMAINED THERE UNTIL THE FIRST YEAR OF KING CYRUS.

Dan 1:18-21 NIV

After that, Daniel still kept operating with the currency of excellence. In his excellence, he was able to provide answers to a knotty issue when none of the wise men in the land could even fathom a way out. That is another fruit of an excellent spirit. It produces exceptional results in the face of difficulty. The King needed help remembering his dreams and also interpreting it. None of the wise men, magicians or enchanters in the whole of Babylon could come up with the answer. They told the king that no one on earth could ever do that for him, except he was a god.

The astrologers answered the king, "THERE IS NOT A MAN ON EARTH WHO CAN DO WHAT THE KING ASKS! No king, however great and mighty, has ever asked such a thing of any magician or enchanter or astrologer. WHAT THE KING ASKS IS TOO DIFFICULT. No one can reveal it to the king except the gods, and they do not live among men."

Dan 2:10-11 NIV

These astrologers who were on the king's payroll showcased their ordinariness to the king when they told him that what he had requested was too difficult. The king had probably spent a fortune furnishing them with the best gadgets for astrology thinking that when he came to a difficult situation, they would read the skies and proffer excellent solutions. But when such a critical moment came, they could not perform above what the ordinary astrologer could do. The truth is, excellence supersedes the use of instruments that were made by imperfect men. Remember that excellence is a state of possessing good qualities in extraordinary measures. It is the quality that makes one outstanding in such a manner that far surpasses the normal standards. The quality of excellence is what makes a man exceptional at everything he does. This currency of excellence however was lacking in the king's astrologers. To be excellent at what you do, you need to know more than the instruments you use. You need to have a greater source from which you draw wisdom, insight and inspiration. This is because many times, your instruments would fail and what you have learned in school may also fail. Even in the field of academic discovery, the most excellent researchers and academicians are those who have been able to look beyond what is already known and tap into the unknown. That is an aptitude that is far above the normal standards of learning. To be able to achieve that requires a mind that is willing to challenge the status quo and not accept the general norm for an answer. That was what king Nebuchadnezzar was looking for. He was looking for an answer that was above the norm. He needed something higher that only an excellent mind could provide. And the only way that high class information could be accessed was by rubbing minds with the most excellent Mastermind in the planet known as the Holy Spirit. Like was earlier established, the Holy Spirit is the Spirit of Excellence. Now Daniel stepped in and proved to all the wise men and astrologers in the province of Babylon that any man who fellowships with the Spirit of excellence becomes a god wherever he steps into.

During the night the mystery was revealed to Daniel in a

vision. Then Daniel praised the God of heaven and said: "Praise be to the name of God forever and ever; wisdom and power are his.

Dan 2:19-20 NIV

Now after Daniel conveys the mysterious dream and its interpretation to Nebuchadnezzar, what follows is a dramatic turn of events. The excellence of Daniel's communication and the detailing of both the dream and its interpretation made the king put his ego aside and acknowledge the God of Daniel. The excellent way Daniel explained both the dream and its interpretation threw the king off his royal throne. It was so serious that the king did not know when he lost his comportment and royal pride. First thing the king does is to prostrate before Daniel in honour of him and his excellent God. Isn't that funny? For a king to prostrate before a man who is a captive from another nation; it definitely means that this man is not an ordinary person. No king ever prostrates before anyone no matter what he has achieved or accomplished. They are trained and raised to exude royalty, charisma and comportment. Every king has an air of royalty around him and nothing excites kings easily. They were born in so much wealth, royalty and opulence that nothing easily baffles them. But when excellence is displayed, no matter the training or resistance, it cannot be ignored even by kings.

Many men and women of the black race scattered around the world always complain of being marginalized because of their skin colour. A United Kingdom based Nigerian Professor named Chris Imafidon got to the attention of the Queen of England when his kids were reported to have displayed excellence in academics. The Queen's granddaughter had told her that the GCSE exam was so difficult. The next morning as Queen Elizabeth II was reading the newspaper, she read about a little girl who had passed that very exam at primary school. This was the exam that her 17-year-old granddaughter said was so hard. The Queen was marveled! She asked how it happened and they told her that the child was a genius. She then asked them to go and look for the father of that excellent child. She did not care whether he was black or white skinned. Her father who was Professor Imafidon never even knew that the Queen could like a black man like him. But because of the excellence that was displayed by his children, she gave them an award and became interested in knowing how they were able to do what everybody found so difficult. This man named Professor Chris Imafidon is a world renowned adviser to governments, presidents and royalties. In an interview with Nonye Ben, he made a remarkable statement when asked if he was facing any kind of segregation in the United Kingdom. He said, "There is no racism. I can tell you clearly. Anytime they see talent, they forget about your colour. They come here to look for Nwankwo Kanu to come and play football for Arsenal. He is not from London, so why did they give him that opportunity to play for them and they paid him millions of pounds even more than the Arsenal boys who were there before him? Talent lifts you above geographical boundaries or even racial boundaries. I am not supposed to have access to the Queen of England but a goldfish has no hiding place. The Queen read about how the kids were doing in school and requested to see me".[2] How true! When any man discovers his talent and hones it to become exceptional and excellent, his skin colour whether white, red or black, would not matter. It would be totally forgotten and considered irrelevant. That was what happened in the case of Daniel. The verses below show how Daniel was given yet another juicy appointment in Babylon without any application.

THEN KING NEBUCHADNEZZAR FELL PROSTRATE BEFORE DANIEL AND PAID HIM HONOR AND ORDERED THAT AN OFFERING AND INCENSE BE PRESENTED TO HIM. The king said to Daniel, "Surely your God is the God of gods and the Lord of kings and a revealer of mysteries, for you were able to reveal this mystery." THEN THE KING PLACED DANIEL IN A HIGH POSITION and lavished many gifts on him. HE MADE HIM RULER OVER THE ENTIRE PROVINCE OF BABYLON AND PLACED HIM IN CHARGE OF ALL ITS WISE MEN.

Dan 2:46-49 NIV

Notice that all Daniel did to land the best job in the empire was that he proposed to offer a solution to an obvious problem. If you want to get the best job in any establishment or sector of society, you too can use that same approach and you would be amazed at the kind of results you would get. Look in and around the establishment, parastatal, company or organization and find out what the problems are. Find out if what they are doing can be improved upon or whether you can double or triple the kind of results they are getting. After you have done your research and have understudied the system, come up with solutions to all the problems you spotted, both the obvious ones and the ones that are not obvious. After doing that, write all of these problems and the solutions you would offer if given the chance. Attach your contact information to the document and find a way to get that proposal to the hands of the decision makers in that system where you want to add value. The moment that document gets to the right hands, and they go through it, discovering that you have a proposal that would add excellent value to them, they would immediately request your services. That was what Daniel did.

There was yet another event that took place and this time a new king needed a consultant to come and interpret a problem and find a possible solution. His name was King Belshazzar, son of King Nebuchadnezzar.

Suddenly the fingers of a human hand appeared and wrote on the plaster of the wall, near the lampstand in the royal palace. The king watched the hand as it wrote. His face turned pale and he was so frightened that his knees knocked together and his legs gave way. The king called out for the enchanters, astrologers and diviners to be brought and said to these wise men of Babylon, "Whoever reads this writing and tells me what it means will be clothed in purple and have a gold chain placed around his neck, and he will be made the third highest ruler in the kingdom.

Dan 5:5-7 NIV

As usual, the astrologers, enchanters and diviners could not provide the wisdom needed to solve the problem. It would take a man who had the currency of wisdom, understanding and excellence to proffer the solution. The king grew pale and worried when they could not find anyone to interpret the handwriting on the wall. That was when the queen came in and mentioned Daniel's excellent record to him. She made a referral and recommended Daniel for the contract. After interpreting it with excellent detailing Daniel bagged another top notch position to become the third highest ruler in Babylon, an office he never applied for.

Inasmuch as an EXCELLENT SPIRIT, knowledge, understanding, interpreting dreams, solving riddles, and explaining enigmas were found in this Daniel, whom the king named Belteshazzar, NOW LET DANIEL BE CALLED,

AND HE WILL GIVE THE INTERPRETATION. Then Daniel was brought in before the king. The king spoke, and said to Daniel, "Are you that Daniel who is one of the captives from Judah, whom my father the king brought from Judah? I HAVE HEARD OF YOU, THAT THE SPIRIT OF GOD is in you, and that light and understanding and EXCELLENT wisdom are found in you. Now the wise men, the astrologers, have been brought in before me, that they should read this writing and make known to me its interpretation, BUT THEY COULD NOT GIVE THE INTERPRETATION OF THE THING. And I have heard of you, that you can give interpretations and explain enigmas. Now if you can read the writing and make known to me its interpretation, you shall be clothed with purple and have a chain of gold around your neck, AND SHALL BE THE THIRD RULER IN THE KINGDOM."

Dan 5:12-16 NKJV

As though this was not enough, Daniel yet increased in the currency of excellence such that the next king who ascended the throne after Belshazzar noticed Daniel. This is because Daniel had established himself as a brand by reason of his excellence. Whenever a new Managing Director assumes office in an establishment, the first set of people who catch his attention through excellent practice and exceptional qualities are those who have established themselves as a brand. You are first a brand as a person before your career or business brand comes into play. A brand speaks of what people know a particular person, company, its products and services for. It takes the currency of excellence to develop a brand. Branding is the art of discovering your unique value which sets you apart from every other person, product, service or business. Branding also entails promoting your value, strengths and uniqueness in order to generate a greater public awareness. You must distinguish yourself as a brand if you want to land the best jobs and contracts. When you are distinguished, you stand out by excellence.

> **Now Daniel so DISTINGUISHED HIMSELF among the administrators and the satraps BY HIS EXCEPTIONAL QUALITIES that the king planned to set him over the whole kingdom.**
> *Dan 6:3 NIV*

Those who employ the services of staffs and workers do not want to be on a constant lookout, monitoring every detail of their duty because that is what they were employed for in the first place. If the employer has to always check on the person he employed to ensure he does the work he is paid to do then something is wrong. He might as well do the work himself or employ someone more competent to do an excellent job. I gave a contract to a man one time and had the worst experience all my life. He offered to do a job for me at a favourable bargain and promised to deliver excellent services to me at that price. He also promised to meet my two weeks deadline for the delivery of the job. Since this was my first job with him, I decided to monitor this contractor to see that I get the delivery in record time by calling him and checking him up from time to time. Whenever I called him, he would tell me all was working fine and everything was moving on in proper schedule. Several days to the deadline for that job to be completed, I decided to pay him a surprise visit so that I could see for myself how far the job had progressed. That was when I received the shock of my life. This young man had not even made the progress he had always spoken to me about on phone whenever I called him. He actually neglected my job and started doing other people's jobs so that he could make more money off the other people. I had already given him a 70 percent downpayment for the job but yet he shoved it aside to take on other jobs in a bid to get more money for himself while delaying my job. When I discovered this I was in utter disappointment and I decided to stay with him from morning till night just to ensure he does my job. He would do my job and after sometime go on to start doing another person's job until I would confront him and insist he focuses on my job. He was highly unprofessional in his approach to my work and his customer service standard was at its lowest ebb. At some point, because I knew that he was already tending towards not meeting up with the agreed deadline, I decided to start doing some bit of the work I had paid this young man to do, just so that my work could go on. I did that for three consecutive days in order to monitor that my work not only gets to completion but also gets delivered exactly when it was needed for market distribution. Each day, when I get back home late in the night, I would feel so stressed, devastated and disappointed because I was doing a work I had paid someone else to deliver on. At the end of the day, he did not meet my deadline and did not also deliver the quality and exact quantity of what I had bargained for. I regretted ever giving him the contract in the first place. His price regime had attracted me, but his lack of professionalism and excellence had caused me to never recommend him to anyone, nor give him any contracts ever again.

The next contract I gave out which was of a similar nature was given out to someone else. This person was given a ten days deadline, but delivered the job in five days. He had many other jobs to attend to from many different customers but because of his excellence, he was able to attend to each and every one of them properly. That causes them to bring more jobs and contracts to him. He performed my job with more class, taste and quality. I did not have to even call him to monitor the job. Whenever I tried to check on him, he would reassure me and tell me not to worry. It was not more than five days when he called me to come and pick up my job. I was awestruck at his delivery quality and pace. His job was so excellent and professional. He did not give me one bit of stress. By reason of his excellence, I gave him two other bigger jobs and linked him to different potential customers who were also attracted to the excellence of the job he did for me. If you had a job and two contractors, each representing the same attitude of these two different young men, who would you give it to? Your guess is as good as mine! You would give it to the one who was excellent and more professional. The excellent contractor on the other hand does not need to try to apply for more jobs of that nature from me. His excellence has already spoken on his behalf. As long as he maintains that standard of excellence and professionalism, he would remain booked with more profitable jobs and contracts most of which he did not even apply for.

Building a Global Business Brand with the Currency of Excellence

- **You need excellent team players**

There is a famous saying that the strength of every chain is equivalent to the strength of its weakest link. The same can be said for a business or company that operates with the currency of excellence. The excellence of every establishment is equivalent to the excellence of its least excellent staff. The quality of a football team is in direct proportion to the quality of players in the team. The truth is that you cannot develop people who lack innate potential in the area you want to cultivate excellence in them. Even the king of Babylon, when he wanted to train people who would stand in his palace, sought for people who already had potential for excellence in the areas he needed them to display competence. That notwithstanding, having excellent individual players is not enough to build a team. This is so because individual skills can be a disaster if the individuals do not harness their skills together as a team. You can have the best football stars on a team and yet not win the league if each of those players do not imbibe team spirit and become team players. David leveraged on the excellence of his individual employees to build such an excellent company of soldiers. They were not just excellent individually but were also excellent team players. They knew how to watch out for each other's back.

These are the names of David's mighty men: Josheb-Basshebeth, a Tahkemonite, was chief of the Three; HE RAISED HIS SPEAR AGAINST EIGHT HUNDRED MEN, WHOM HE KILLED IN ONE ENCOUNTER. Next to him was Eleazar son of Dodai the Ahohite. As one of the three mighty men, he was with David when they taunted the Philistines gathered [at Pas Dammim] for battle. THEN THE MEN OF ISRAEL RETREATED, BUT HE STOOD HIS GROUND AND STRUCK DOWN THE PHILISTINES TILL HIS HAND GREW TIRED AND FROZE TO THE SWORD. THE LORD BROUGHT ABOUT A GREAT VICTORY THAT DAY. THE TROOPS RETURNED TO ELEAZAR, BUT ONLY TO STRIP THE DEAD. Next to him was Shammah son of Agee the Hararite. WHEN THE PHILISTINES BANDED TOGETHER AT A PLACE WHERE THERE WAS A FIELD FULL OF LENTILS, ISRAEL'S TROOPS FLED FROM THEM. BUT SHAMMAH TOOK HIS STAND IN

THE MIDDLE OF THE FIELD. HE DEFENDED IT AND STRUCK THE PHILISTINES DOWN, AND THE LORD BROUGHT ABOUT A GREAT VICTORY.
2 Sam 23:8-19 NIV

It would interest you to know that the mighty men of valour who contributed to David's excellent brand as an undefeated company of warriors did not start out as mighty men. David's company had a lot of exceptional staffs that were raised by him. They were thirty seven in number according to scripture (2 Sam 23:39). Among these thirty seven exceptionally excellent staffs of his, David had three high ranking officers under his employ who were extremely exceptional and extraordinarily excellent. They were so proficient that one of them killed eight hundred men at a time. The other two single handedly took down troops and bands of Philistine army on separate occasions. Having a man who can take down eight hundred men with a spear on one encounter on your staffing as an army commander is no joke. It is like having a Samson on your team as a commander.

ABISHAI the brother of Joab son of Zeruiah was CHIEF OF THE THREE. HE RAISED HIS SPEAR AGAINST THREE HUNDRED MEN, WHOM HE KILLED, and so he became as famous as the Three. Was he not held in greater honor than the Three? He became their commander, even though he was not included among them. BENAIAH son of Jehoiada was a valiant fighter from Kabzeel, who performed great exploits. HE STRUCK DOWN TWO OF MOAB'S BEST MEN. HE ALSO WENT DOWN INTO A PIT ON A SNOWY DAY AND KILLED A LION. AND HE STRUCK DOWN A HUGE EGYPTIAN. ALTHOUGH THE EGYPTIAN HAD A SPEAR IN HIS HAND, BENAIAH WENT AGAINST HIM WITH A CLUB. HE SNATCHED THE SPEAR FROM THE EGYPTIAN'S HAND

AND KILLED HIM WITH HIS OWN SPEAR. Such were the exploits of Benaiah son of Jehoiada; he too was as famous as the three mighty men. He was held in greater honor than any of the Thirty, but he was not included among the Three. AND DAVID PUT HIM IN CHARGE OF HIS BODYGUARD.
2 Sam 23:18-23 NIV

They were initially ordinary men who had lost hope and enthusiasm. They were broke, and out of jobs, they needed to make a difference in their lives. They came to David to align with him and possibly get admitted into his company. David accepted them, but did not leave them that way. He trained them and built into them the quality of excellence both by association and by instruction. The result was a band of mighty men who became so excellent and professional in their dealings. By reason of their individual excellence, David's company became extraordinary on a corporate level.

- **You need an excellent team**

Building a globally relevant business brand requires an excellent team. Raising an excellent team from the scratch can be a very tough and challenging task. This is because people are prone to bring everything about who they are into the business, company or team. When people come into your business, company or firm, they come in with their opinions, knowledge, past work experiences, upbringing, education, prior team experiences, life challenges and family issues. And you do not want this to have a negative impact on your business brand because bad news spreads faster than good news. It takes time to build an excellent reputation but absolutely no time to destroy and tarnish one that was once renowned for excellence. David was faced with this challenge, and he knew that excellence in teamwork and collaboration can be taught and developed. He therefore was able to raise an excellent team that made his company of warriors a very formidable and unconquerable one.

A team consists of different uniquely gifted and talented people who have a common purpose and have complementary skills. Team members work together, share common goals and try to pool individual skills and expertise together in order to bring a business to the next level. Members of a team work with the mentality that everyone either succeeds together or fails together. When one team member needs help, the other stands in to offer him the needed assistance.

David left Gath and escaped to the cave of Adullam. When his brothers and his father's household heard about it, they went down to him there. All those who were in distress or in debt or discontented gathered around him, and he became their leader. About four hundred men were with him.

1 Sam 22:1-2 NIV

In a team that is making progress, what you find is a leader who does not just sit back and dole out orders but works with the team to get the job done. If you want your business to succeed, then you need help from people you can trust with your dreams of success. In other words, if you want to build a global business brand, you must have excellent people around you as employees, board of trustees, facilitators, managers, marketers, sales personnel, etc. Building a business that becomes of global relevance transcends beyond just having a clear idea of where the business should be in the future. Global reckoning in a business brand can only come by making your business or company one that would be known for excellence at every stage of its growth. This standard of excellence is not one that can be achieved by a one man show or by just one man's excellence. To establish any kind of business with a globally competitive edge in its industry, all the players involved must also contribute their own due quota of the currency of excellence required. David built a global brand out of nothing. His army never lost any battle because David invested himself heavily on his team. He poured out himself into them until they began to function in a frequency of excellence as high as his. This is something most owners of businesses and Chief Executive Officers of organizations find difficult to do hence their companies and businesses stagnate at a particular level for so long. They fail to know the importance of a team, let alone strengthening every individual within their team structure.

- **You need excellent staffs**

For your business to grow, everyone including your staffs has to get better, from the top executives to the lowest cadre of staffs. You must ensure excellence in all levels of staffs including the men at the gate or the security men. This is important because that has a way of speaking to people about your brand. When people step into your office, business place or establishment, everything speaks to them. From the way your security man receives them into the premises, to the way each of your staffs addresses them. These people are picking signals and messages both subtly or deliberately. It is not about you as the pioneer, founder or overseer just being great. You must commit to their personal improvement on an individual level. They are the building blocks of your enterprise hence they must be strong and excellent if your enterprise would be strong and excellent. Someone once said, "If you would build a strong house then you must build strong bricks". You must get to know your staffs or foundation members on an individual level. Invest in them and commit to them developing into more resourceful members of your establishment. Help them discover their strengths and build on it. Help them learn, help them grow in such a way that they can stand in for you when you are in need of support or when you need them to handle some major tasks.

When she (the Queen of Sheba) discovered how wise he really was, and how breathtaking the beauty of his palace, and how wonderful the food at his tables, and how many servants and aides he had, AND WHEN SHE SAW THEIR SPECTACULAR UNIFORMS AND HIS STEWARDS IN FULL REGALIA, AND SAW THE SIZE OF THE MEN IN HIS BODYGUARD, SHE COULD SCARCELY BELIEVE IT!

2 Chron 9:3-4 TLB

Solomon was a Chief Executive Officer who invested heavily on the staff in his company. By reason of the wisdom and excellence he injected into his empire, he became a global brand. His name went as far as the East with no technology, no social media, no camera nor any medium for instant communication and spread. His kingdom and business empire went viral such that even in the East, it was the talk on the lips of all and that caught the attention of the Queen of Sheba. When she came, she saw the excellence of Solomon's servants, stewards and staffs and was marveled at the excellence of his royalty. Mind you, the Queen of Sheba was herself royalty. For these details to catch her attention in such a unique way, it means it was extraordinarily and exceptionally breathtaking. The fact that Solomon's excellence dazzled the imaginations of other kings and queens proves that his excellence was a product of the workings of the Spirit of Excellence through him and not a function of his wealth.

Keys to Converting the Currency of Excellence into Tangible Wealth

- **Be yourself**

If you want to achieve excellence in business and career, you must first identify your areas of strength and competitive advantage. When talking about excellence, the first thing to consider is that it is already coded in you. As you are, with all the imperfections you may have, you still have within you great potentials to excel in life. All you need is to sharpen and chisel off those imperfections to bring out the best in you. That is why you must accept yourself the way you are and not wish you were someone else because that person appears excellent. It means you do not have to become someone else in order to achieve excellence. All you need do is to become yourself. Because inherent in every kingdom citizen is the capacity for excellence. But in order to become the real you on the outside, you would need to identify the skills, talents, abilities, strengths and gifting that comes naturally to you. Everybody has gifts and talents and would make the most progress when they go in the direction of excelling at what comes easily to them. That is the area where you can derive absolute fulfillment and satisfaction. To achieve this you must learn never to compare yourself with other people. Never measure your progress by the results other people are getting. Just become more like yourself every day. That is, allow the real you which is inside gain constant refinement and improvement. Commit yourself deliberately to always learn new things by self education or formal education. When you do this intentionally you would always be developing yourself to be the very best version of you. As you do, your excellence and uniqueness would become more pronounced and soon enough, you would begin to experience the results that only excellence commands. Therefore look within and begin to pull out all the gems locked in the inside of you. Shut yourself out from external influences that try to tilt you towards trying to be like someone else.

- **Become the best at what you do.**

The moment you discover the area in business or career you want to venture into, you must make a resolve in your heart to become the best at it. Commit yourself to excellence because that is what differentiates the extraordinary people from the ordinary. That little extra effort they make to be excellent at what they do is what births exceptional results. But complacence, laziness or a lack of motivation destroys a lot of potentials and hinders their inborn greatness from gaining full expression. *If you do not have enough motivation or passion to fuel your drive towards excellence, it could be that you are not on the right path or calling*. But when you are in the right vocation for which you were made, you would easily be motivated to embark on the journey of excellence. You would always seek for better ways to do things and source for new ways to achieve results. That would spur you on to self education. You would begin to surf for knowledge on that field by reading books, listening to programs that would drive you closer to being the best and attending seminars, trainings and workshops. As you do this, you would gain more excellence and would be abreast of the best practices that have come into the limelight in your particular industry. Be hungry for information that would propel you in your journey to excellence. Read everything you can find on your business or industry. Study about those who have achieved excellence in their life's journey by reading their stories, books and articles about them. The more you learn about your profession, your trade, your art, your course of study and your craft, the more confident you will become in your ability to do it well.

▪ Do not be afraid of mistakes

Professor Chris Imafidon who is a Nigerian based in the United Kingdom is famed for being the father of the brainiest kids in the world. The names of his kids even got into the Guinness book of records as the world's smartest kids. This came about as a result of the fact that his three kids passed the GCSE exams in primary school each at very young age. This exam is usually meant to test the knowledge of secondary school students. But his three daughters, at their primary school level, passed the exams despite their extremely young ages. It was reported that his first, second and third daughter passed the exam at the age of eleven, nine and six respectively. His third daughter at six even scored double what her elder sisters scored when they wrote the same exams years before. Nobody had ever had two siblings from the same family with such an excellent result. So immediately they saw this, his kids were awarded honours for being the brainiest kids in the world. When Professor Chris Imafidon was interviewed and asked how he was able to raise, teach and develop his kids to be so excellent, he made some profound statements. He said, "Buy your kids toy instruments. Let them ruin them if they must. It sounds very expensive anyway but you are teaching the child more than any book because the child is doing it, knowing it and fixing it. My children ruined a lot of my computers when they were growing up. I was so annoyed. But all that they ruined made them understand the internal workings of the devices. When my girl went to school, the school computer crashed. The head teacher's Personal Assistant called the technical support team to come and fix it. My daughter came in, saw the screen with the error message and said she could fix it since it was the same message that was on the one she fixed at home. She was able to fix it instantly and it started working. When the engineer came, they told him a little girl had fixed it. He insisted on seeing my daughter. She told him what she did to the computer and the man opened his wallet and gave her 20 pounds! She was seven years then. The man looked at the head teacher and other staff members and told them if they had problems with their computers, they should call my daughter first before calling him".[2] If he had not swallowed the pains of allowing his children develop their skills, they may never have discovered themselves that early. They developed their skills by learning from their mistakes with his gadgets and sometimes damaging them in the process. His daughter went on to attract several academic honours for her excellence and service to humanity including an MBE in the year 2016. She achieved all of these by reason of the currency of excellence. And it began with her father allowing her to make some mistakes with his computers and sometimes ruining them in her curiosity.

⌐ Develop new skill and improve on old ones.

When you develop new skills in your given area of strength, you would discover that you would become better at what you do. You would also notice that you have become difficult to substitute or replace whether you work in an organization or you run a business. Your customers would be held spell bound to your goods and services because you are always improving. That is the place every business and career professional would be when he commits to excellence by constant improvement of his skills. There are some people in organizations who are never considered when the management is trying to cut down on its workforce. These are people who are multitalented in their field and are always ahead when it comes to excellent performance. ***When you expand your skill base, you would discover that your value would increase before the eyes of your customers and your business competitors.*** Your boss would find it difficult not to notice you and would try hard to ensure that you do not leave for a better offer in another establishment. They would do their best to keep you even if it means giving you a raise. You would also increase the demand that would be placed on you because you have gained experience in a wide range of skills. The easy way to develop a new skill or improve on an old one is by habitual performance or habitual practice. ***Any skill is learnable if you put your mind to it and desire to excel in the use of that skill in performing your job.*** You can learn any skill you need to learn to achieve any goal that you can set for yourself as long as it is within your range of core competence. For example, if you are in the information technology industry, you would be better off learning the use of newer software packages. The more skillful you are with a variety of software applications that are relevant both directly and indirectly to your field the more valuable you would become in that industry. The Bible shows us how Solomon needed to build several structures with bronze metal. He had to go get someone from outside his kingdom, as far as Tyre. He got this young man called Hiram, and gave him a contract to perform all his jobs. Mind you, Hiram never sought for this contract, but it seemed that he was the only one who was skilled in all kinds of bronze work. That gave him the leverage over all the workmen in Israel and he was contracted to do the job. This man got just one contract that turned his fortune around because he was highly skilled and had developed himself in all kinds of bronze work. By virtue of his vast range of skills in that area, he did a lot of different works of construction for King Solomon on the same project. Some of the many different structures which Hiram made for Solomon were mentioned in the book of 1 Kings 7:15-47.

King Solomon sent to Tyre and brought Huram, whose mother was a widow from the tribe of Naphtali and whose father was a man of Tyre and a craftsman in bronze. HURAM WAS HIGHLY SKILLED AND EXPERIENCED IN ALL KINDS OF BRONZE WORK. He came to King Solomon and did all the work assigned to him.
1 Kings 7:13-14 NIV

Many people give up on developing new skills in their areas of passion because when they first tried functioning there, it did not come out perfect. The truth is that life is not perfect; neither is excellence a call to perfectness. Excellence is more about growing and maturing in a given direction by becoming better at every count. That does not mean you would get it right on your first attempt at doing what you are gifted for. As you develop new skills, you must not be afraid of making mistakes because if you never make any mistake it means you have never tried anything worthwhile. Excellence is a journey and when you see it that way, you would succeed in anything you approach; especially when it is approached with a commitment to daily improvement.

▪ Always deliver excellent services

It has long been proven that companies with high quality performance, products and services can charge more and earn more per sale because they deliver excellence. A commitment to product or service excellence is the safest and most predictable strategy for achieving business success. If you want to make a difference in anything you do, you must know that offering excellent services is not negotiable. A lot of people undermine its importance and have their businesses gradually grinding to a halt. Many people have lost their careers due to their mediocre approach to work. There are many incompetent trained professionals who ruin people's lives every day with their mediocre services. In the engineering field, when a major failure in anything that was supervised or built by an engineer occurs, investigations are carried out. If it is discovered that the failure occurred because the engineer who supervised the design or built the structure was grossly incompetent, that engineer could lose his license. His incompetence can be seen as a product of lack of the currency of excellence. There are many doctors who have lost their medical license and hence their careers because of the kind of mediocre services they have rendered to some clients. There are also Pharmacists who have received promotions they never imagined due to their excellent customer service.

I know of a Pharmaceutical doctor who was once working as a locum staff in a pharmacy during his compulsory youth service in Abuja, Nigeria. By some string of events, he treated a young boy who was brought to the Pharmacy where he works and the boy became well. When the mother of that boy heard about the excellent service this Pharm. Dr. rendered to her son, she went to the pharmacy in search for this young man. This lady asked after the Pharm. Dr. and when she saw him, she asked him if he wanted a job. Remember, this young man was just doing his one year Nigeria Youth Service Corps (NYSC). He had not even started applying for jobs yet. He was waiting to get done with his NYSC before making that move. But because of his excellence, he did not need to look for a job again; the best jobs were now looking for him. *When you possess the currency of excellence you would not be stranded looking around for jobs because jobs would be looking for you no matter the rate of unemployment in that nation.* The woman whose son he had treated gave him a very wonderful job in a Non Governmental Organization (NGO). Guess what! Apart from the incentives and allowances, he became entitled to a basic salary of ₦600,000 (NGN) monthly. Just like that? Yes! For a job he never applied for? Yes! Even though he did not know how this came about, I know from my study of this young man's story, that he had put the currency of excellence to work. This currency was converted into the best job for him with a very good pay for a start. Make providing excellent services with every chance you get a priority, and see the amazing results you would command.

r Bring out the best in others.

Professor Chris Imafidon, the Nigerian-born Professor at the University of Oxford, England, did something very remarkable when he attended a graduation ceremony at the University of Ilorin, Nigeria. This renowned Professor whose children have been described as world's brainiest kids promised that he would give a scholarship to the worst graduating student to the shock of those who witnessed the occasion. When he was asked, he spoke about how his grandmother always believed and taught him that every single child had so much to contribute to the society. This woman of wisdom was interested in every child. In his words, he said, "I did what she would have done", when he was responding to his interviewer. He said he had become a firm believer of the fact that every child is a genius. He said, "If every child is a genius, then it should not matter if you are at the top of the class, bottom or middle". When the lecturers argued with him about giving such an unconventional grant, he told them that they would see what these people they judged as the worst students would become. He insisted on his decision by saying, "I would give them scholarships and if they don't beat the ones you say are the best students after three years, I will publicly apologize". What an audacious statement; This man clearly was committed to helping children and students bring out the genius on the inside of them.

Most times, the school system reject the very people who they were supposed to groom. They choose the best according to their own standards and turn their backs against the geniuses hidden in the so called unintelligent child. If only the educational institutions would learn their lesson and take a cue from Professor Chris Imafidon, they would see that every child has potential to become a genius if properly tutored.

The former Prime Minister of the United Kingdom also doubted the efficacy of Professor Chris' claim. One time, he challenged the Professor with a bet of $25 million (USD) just to prove that his claims were not tenable or attainable, but he lost his money at the end. Professor Chris Imafidon told the former Prime Minister to give him the worst performing schools and the least students in those schools. He was going to work with these so called least students for nine months after which they would be tested with the best students in the best schools. David Cameron laughed at the thought as he placed his bet. According to the Professor, when the former English Prime Minister came back nine months later, he could not believe what he saw. The children had been transformed into excellence by rubbing minds with this great Professor. The Professor spoke to the children, mentored them and adopted them as if they were his biological children; he literally took them under his wings. According to the

Professor, he did not even teach them all the subjects. He just spoke to the hidden genius on the inside of them. He spoke to their personality and gave them a new identity. He used one or two subjects as samples to aid their academic prowess and they became so brilliant that in one year, they beat the best student from the best school. The Professor won the challenge and used the money to build a school in Birmingham.

NOTE: This story is used to encourage you to become creative in thinking of ways to bring out the best in the rejected. It is not stated to support or encourage betting or gambling in anyway.

CHARGE
Excellence would always find you out. The quality of your life would be in direct proportion to your level of excellence regardless of your chosen field of endeavor. When you display excellence in anything you do, there is a great chance that you would always be considered by the decision makers when fresh opportunities are available. You can get a contract you never sought for or a job you never applied for by this virtue called excellence. As you commit to excellence you would become better at what you do and you would be a better version of yourself. Your uniqueness is strongly connected to how excellently you can display your God given potential in whatever endeavour you decide to embark on. Be known for excellence in all you do and the world would seek you in due time.

AFFIRMATIONS
I am excellent because the Spirit of Excellence resides in me. I deliver excellence in everything I do. My business is excellent and I work with excellent people at my job. I walk

in excellence because I possess the currency of excellence. I add excellent value everywhere I go and I receive excellent rewards for my value daily. I grow in excellence daily, becoming better at what I do every day.

FOOD FOR THOUGHTS

- Excellence in spirit is an attitude which is cultivated by virtue of the interactions we have with the Holy Spirit as kingdom species.

- Your best promotional tool for marketing is your excellent service or excellent product.

- When you expand your skill base, you would discover that your value would increase before the eyes of your customers and your business competitors.

- Any skill is learnable if you put your mind to it and desire to excel in the use of that skill in performing your job.

- When you possess the currency of excellence you would not be stranded looking around for jobs because jobs would be looking for you no matter the rate of unemployment in that nation.

CHAPTER TWO
THE CURRENCY OF VISION

"Many people are working for money. That's an inferior reason to work. We must work for the vision within us."

Dr. Myles Munroe - International Speaker

Every human on this planet is born with a vision that may appear unknown to him at birth. As growth takes place and consciousness is awakened to the environment, each individual is expected to begin to get a glimpse of his personal God-given vision for life and for his destiny. No human being was born to tread the globe without having a clear-cut vision to fulfill. The extent to which your vision covers is the boundary within which you can experience any truly notable accomplishment. To achieve excellence in any area of life, whether academics, business, career, family, etc, you need vision. A lot of people are stagnated in their career because they have never envisioned what they want to achieve. By reason of this, they are tossed to and fro not knowing exactly what they want. Many businesses are grounded today because there is no clear cut vision in view. Without vision in career and business, you may never be able to make a difference. Most people think vision is only useful when one wants to establish a church ministry. But they could not be further from the truth. Whether you are involved in ministry, academics, business or career, you need to have a vision for your life if you would accomplish what God has in store for you.

What is Vision?
Vision is the picture of a desired future which has been preordained for an individual to capture, with the telescope of his mind. When vision is in view, motion becomes properly directed and direction becomes goal oriented. Vision is the ability to see beyond the present into an expected end. Vision thrives on the power of imagination at work in an individual. Vision causes one to know where he is going and gives such a person an automatic compass that guides his journey toward the prescribed destination. Vision is strengthened by focused imagination which is channeled toward the fulfillment of a goal.

Life without a vision in place and in view would be reduced to a haphazard and erratic motion. Such a person would simply just run around in circles. This kind of life is driven and propelled only by the opinions and suggestions of men. A man who lacks vision would be at the mercy of the approval of men. He would trade his individuality for another man's personality. He would make another man's vision his dream and pursue after another man who may just be running his own race without catching up. But life with a vision is a smooth ride, with orderly and consistent upward and forward motion. Without vision, motion is a catastrophic adventure which ends the visionless pilot in a crash. Vision births focus.

Then the Lord said to me, "Write my answer plainly on tablets, so that a runner can carry the correct message to others. THIS VISION IS FOR A FUTURE TIME. IT DESCRIBES THE END, AND IT WILL BE FULFILLED. IF IT SEEMS SLOW IN COMING, WAIT PATIENTLY, FOR IT WILL SURELY TAKE PLACE. IT WILL NOT BE DELAYED.
Hab 2:2-4 NLT

Vision propels motion and the wonderful thing about vision which people do not understand is that you do not have to have it all figured out before you move forward in a vision oriented direction.

Purpose and Vision

There is a thin line of distinction between vision and purpose. This is largely due to the fact that they both go hand in hand and hence possess great similarities. Purpose is the mother of vision because it precedes vision. Without purpose, there can be no clear-cut vision and as a matter of fact, purpose is the bedrock upon which every high standing vision is founded. Purpose is the "why" of your existence while vision is the "where" of your destination. *That is, purpose beggars the question: "why am I here?", while vision triggers the question "where am I going?"* Purpose reveals the essence of your existence while vision reveals the scope of your existence. Purpose is the reason for being, while vision is the picture of haven become what you were purposed to be. In order for vision to be thoroughly grasped, purpose must be seriously understood. No one becomes excellent in anything without a preconceived vision of accomplishing mastery and excellence. Every individual on the planet has a purpose and needs to live it out in order to experience true fulfillment. Without a discovery of self in view of purpose, satisfaction would remain a myth. But when a man lives a life of purpose, fulfillment becomes his everyday experience as he makes progress toward making his vision a reality. Many people have extraneous dreams which are really not founded on the platform of purpose. What they have are but mere illusions of grandeur and vague wishes for a better tomorrow. Many students get into school without a purpose conscious approach. They get in just to join the bandwagon of those who seem to be headed toward the direction of pursuing a certificate without any real interest in gaining advancement through knowledge. While schooling is a big necessity for formal education and for all who intend to learn in a more organized fashion, schooling without purpose could have very little impact on a given student. It could even lead to frustration if not properly handled and checked. Conversely, schooling on purpose could make a great world of difference because it makes learning deliberate, in a manner that brings about the fulfillment of one's vision.

I read a story of a young promising doctor who had just

graduated with flying colours. He had been called up to the stage to receive an award for his outstanding performance and distinguished service to the community where he served. His parents were in that auditorium, full of pride, satisfaction and a sense of fulfillment as their son received the awards. The father had always dreamed of becoming a medical doctor but could not. While this boy was still young, his father did all he could to get him to become a medical doctor and this ceremony was proof that his father had succeeded in getting his wish come to pass. As this doctor mounted the podium, and the applause subsided, the doctor began to give his speech. He said, "Please Mom and Dad, forgive me, I am sorry I cannot go on." With embarrassment they all left the event and on their way home he explained to them. He said, "Everything I have ever achieved during these years have been done to please you Dad, and to fulfill your lifelong dreams." Despite the cars, the houses and other material things he had acquired he still did not feel fulfilled because he did not follow his dreams and visions. Purpose is God's original intent, while vision on the other hand is man's perception of God's intended desire for his existence. Purpose can only be found when the original intent for which something was created is discovered.

Napoleon Hill, in his bestseller "Think and Grow Rich", said, "Never has there been so great an opportunity for practical dreamers as now exists. We should be encouraged to know that this dynamic world in which we live is demanding new ideas, new ways of doing things, new leaders, new inventions, new methods of teaching, new methods of marketing, new books, new literature, new applications for computers, new cures for diseases and new approaches to every aspect of business and life. Behind this demand for new and better things, there is one quality one must possess to win and that is definiteness of purpose, the knowledge of what one wants, and a burning desire to possess it".[1] When you have a vision, you are able to see clearly what you want until the vision possesses you. When your vision possesses you, it turns you crazy and makes people think you are mad because you see pictures they do not see and hear sounds they do not hear. In due time, it would be obvious that you were neither mad, crazy nor in hallucinations but were only possessed by a vision which has now become a reality.

The Vision statement
Everyone who wants to function in excellence in any area of life must develop a personal vision statement. A vision statement is a verbal representation of the picture you have of your future based on the inspiration of the Spirit of God. It is an ironical fact that while most companies have vision statements, individuals who work in such establishments do not have personal vision statements for their lives. Your vision statement is your inspiration, and it gives the framework for all your endeavors. When creating a vision statement, what you are doing is articulating your dreams and hopes for your life based on the specific purpose of God for your life. Your vision statement describes what you are trying to build and serves as a standard for your future actions. Your vision statement also gives a direction for what your core values would entail. A vision statement may apply to an individual, an entire company or even to a single department of that company. Whether it is for an individual, a government or for corporate bodies, a vision statement answers the question, "Where do I (or we) want to go?" This is very critical for excellence to be achieved in both personal and corporate life. Many people do not have a clear vision for their career and hence cannot have a working vision statement. The vision statement is a description of the

destination one intends to reach as a career person or a business owner. The vision statement does not give all the details on how the destination would be reached. It only tells you where exactly you intend to get to. Many people tend to confuse a vision statement with a road map or a blueprint on how to get there. But that is not the purpose for having a vision. That is why many people fail to dream big or see beyond their immediate location or position in life. They allow themselves to be preoccupied with the demands of the immediate such that they are deprived of the possibilities of a bigger and a brighter future. Since your vision statement is not a detailed "roadmap of how" for your small business's future success, it means when you are developing a vision statement there is no harm in allowing your imagination go as far and wide as possible. Take note that a true God given vision cannot be faked. If it is not authentic, there would be no passion to drive the vision. Passion acts like the fuel required to propel you to the destination of your vision. Just like jet fuel burns to project the large aircraft to flight against the force of gravity and inertia. Passion stimulates your motion, your drive, and your speed. When your passion for excellence is intact, you would become like a magnet pulling resources your way. Only a vision generated out of a passion can produce the kind of excellence that can position you for great opportunities that you never bargained for.

WHERE THERE IS NO VISION, THE PEOPLE ARE UNRESTRAINED, but happy is he who keeps the law.
Prov 29:18 NASB

Learn how to write a vision statement for your small business. The Bible says we must write our vision statements and make it plain (Hab 2:2). After writing the vision, learn how to use your vision statement to create an action plan that will help you make the vision for your business or career a reality. A vision statement does not tell you how you are going to get there; it sets the direction for your business planning. That makes crafting a vision statement very critical to the growth of small businesses because the main reason small businesses fail is because of poor planning. Having and being able to articulate and share a vision is one of the qualities of a good businessman. Your vision statement will have a huge influence on decision making and the way you allocate resources once you have it.

The Vision and the Provision

A lot of times, people are always faced with the difficulty of knowing the exact relationship between a vision and the provisions for that vision. By reason of this, many never truly discover their purposes nor even actualize the visions of God for their lives. Many folks are afraid to envision their future because they claim to lack provisions. They feel there is no point having a vision without money or provision to finance the vision. If only they knew that vision in itself was a currency! These folks do not even dare to think big because of the size of their pockets with respect to what is required to sponsor a big idea. In their thinking, every vision would require provision to begin the process of making it become a reality. Vision is God's purpose revealed to man. It is the perception of a God ordained destination. While provision on the other hand, is God's supernatural reward for one's belief in the vision which he received of God. Abraham caught a vision from God where he was showed how great he would become if he gets out of his country to do what God was calling him to do. But provisions came to Abraham as he began to act on the demands of the vision. Most people never have visions for their lives, career or business brand. This is because they tell themselves that they need to have the provisions first before thinking about having a vision. But the sad truth remains that this is not how it works. Thinking that way is like putting the cart before the horse and we already know what outcome to expect of such an arrangement. Because vision itself is a kingdom currency, it is designed to produce provisions for the vision bearer. But that provision would only show up when the vision bearer begins to go about his vision with gusto and enthusiasm. Many potential start-up entrepreneurs have had problems with this principle hence they either dump their ideas or shut their minds totally from receiving great visions. Some others just engage in mere wishful thinking and mistake that for vision.

Most times the reason people have challenges with raising start-up capital is because they think Rome was built in one day. **What you need in order to start developing your vision into a global brand is to think big, plan big, but start small right from where you are. Start with the available resources at hand.** The thing is that most people never admit that they have anything worth starting with. There was a woman whose late husband was indebted and it was going to cost her the two sons she had. She met Elisha the prophet and sought for help. In a bid to offer help to this woman, Elisha asked her what she had. Her response displayed the kind of value she had placed on what she had. She claimed that she had nothing when he asked her for what she had with which wealth could be generated. The problem she had was that she had no value for what she had. No matter who you are, where you are from or what you do, you have something with which you can begin to work on your vision.

The wife of a man from the company of the prophets cried out to Elisha, "Your servant my husband is dead, and you know that he revered the Lord. But now his creditor is coming to take my two boys as his slaves." ELISHA REPLIED TO HER, "HOW CAN I HELP YOU? TELL ME, WHAT DO YOU HAVE IN YOUR HOUSE?" "YOUR SERVANT HAS NOTHING THERE AT ALL," SHE SAID, "EXCEPT A LITTLE OIL." Elisha said, "Go around and ask all your neighbors for empty jars. Don't ask for just a few. Then go inside and shut the door behind you and your sons. Pour oil into all the jars, and as each is filled, put it to one side." She left him and afterward shut the door behind her and her sons. They brought the jars to her and she kept pouring. When all the jars were full, she said to her son, "Bring me another one." But he replied, "There is not a jar left." Then the oil stopped flowing. She went and told the man of God, and he said, "GO, SELL THE OIL AND PAY YOUR DEBTS. YOU AND YOUR SONS CAN LIVE ON WHAT IS LEFT."

2 Kings 4:1-7 NIV

Elisha gave a very high end principle for making provisions available in the above story. **The principle is, look for what you have, find a way to multiply it, go out and sell it, run your business with the proceeds, pay your bills and live on what is left.** If you truly have a vision, one thing that usually follows the conception the vision is passion. Every true vision carries with it a passion and that passion acts like fuel that fires up the vision bearer into doing creative things that he ordinarily would not have thought of, just to get his vision kicking with what is available to him.

The amazing story of Steve Jobs comes to mind whenever the question of start-up capital is considered. Steve Jobs had a vision to get a computer into the hands of everyday people. This man who was the co-founder of the Apple Company and the inventor of the iPhone series, iPod and iPad started the largest technology company in the world in his parents' garage. Steve Jobs started Apple Computers with his partner, Steve Wozniak. The two men did not have a bunch of venture capitalists like startups do today. Jobs had a clear vision coupled with his innovative ideas that helped to catapult Apple into the forefront of the computer industry. On April 1, 1976, the 21-year-old Jobs and Wozniak who was 26 years old at that time formed Apple Computer. This company which happens to be a global tech giant today, started out in Jobs' bedroom and when there was no space left, they set up a shop in Jobs' parents' garage. There they began the globally renowned venture known today as Apple, and began working on the first model of the Apple I. They did not have all the resources they needed but decided to start with what they had. They applied the principle Elisha introduced to the widow woman. They looked within and asked themselves what they had. They took the little they had, sold it and used the money they recovered from it to push their vision further. Most banks were reluctant to lend Jobs money because at that time, the idea of a computer for ordinary people seemed too absurd to comprehend. Steve Jobs was so passionate about this vision that he sold his Volkswagen minibus, while Steve Wozniak sold his Hewlett-Packard calculator. As a result, they were able to generate $1,350 (USD) in capital which they used to start Apple, in the garage of Jobs' parents. As Apple I sold, it brought to them enough cash to enable them modify and improve upon their design and as a result they developed the Apple II in 1977. Apple II was the first personal computer with color graphics and a keyboard. This duo's vision took on the fast lane to success because it produced more user-friendly computers. It turned out to be a tremendous success, ushering in the era of the personal computers. In their first-year alone, sales of Apple II, a product manufactured in a "garage company", as critics would call it, was about $3 million (USD). Just two years later, sales climbed up with a geometric progression and they raked up to $200 million (USD). As of February 9, 2017, Apple Inc was said to be worth an estimated value of $695 billion (USD).[2,3] This company has remained at the forefront of technological advancement even after the demise of Steve Jobs, the man whose vision made a difference for the Apple brand.

BETTER IS THE END OF A THING THAN THE BEGINNING THEREOF: and the patient in spirit is better than the proud in spirit.
Eccl 7:8 KJV

The Bible in the above verse makes us know that it is better to start working on our vision with our mind on the picture of the end. It shows us that this is better than starting with a goal of making the beginning splendid with no end in view. To start a business or enterprise right from where you are with a view of making the future of the enterprise better is vision in progress. It is better to start small and grow big than to start big and grow small.

Vision as a Kingdom Currency

In his book titled, "the Principles and Power of Vision", Dr. Myles Munroe said "Many people are working for money. That's an inferior reason to work. We must work for the vision within us".[4] Most people wake up almost every morning, struggle out of bed, and dash out to a job they hate only because they need the money to pay their bills. But those who have the currency of vision wake up with excitement and go to work with gusto. They are working because of their vision not necessarily because of money. *The interesting part is that money chases after people who work for their*

visions while it runs away from those who work just because of money. When God wants to give a man wealth, He expands that man's visions and broadens his horizon. The bigger the vision a man's mind can conceive; the bigger things his hand would receive in tangible form. Just the way the bigger your bounties are in any known paper currency, the greater the things you can do with your money. The currency of vision has proved to be a necessity for everyday success. God gives everyone vision with which they can make demands on their spiritual bank accounts and that was what He did for Abraham. God wanted to increase Abraham's wealth after his separation from Lot, but the first thing He does is to expand Abraham's vision.

The Lord said to Abram after Lot had parted from him, "LIFT UP YOUR EYES FROM WHERE YOU ARE AND LOOK NORTH AND SOUTH, EAST AND WEST. ALL THE LAND THAT YOU SEE I WILL GIVE TO YOU AND YOUR OFFSPRING FOREVER. I will make your offspring like the dust of the earth, so that if anyone could count the dust, then your offspring could be counted. Go, walk through the length and breadth of the land, for I am giving it to you.

Gen 13:14-17 NIV

Notice what God tells Abraham and how He endows a seventy five year old man with the currency of vision. Abraham had walked through that path before but had probably never lifted up his eyes to see the possibilities he saw when God gave him the vision. He had walked the length and breadth of the land several times before but this time he was doing it with a revelation given him by God. It does not matter how old you are, when God credits you with the currency of vision, your age would not matter at all. As Abraham saw the picture of what God had in store for him, the Bible records that he began to experience a whole new dimension of prosperity.

Achieving Excellence by the Currency of Vision

- **Vision produces power over mediocrity**

Many persons remain mediocre all their life because they lack the currency of vision. Many students go through school and end up average in class and in life because they lack perception of what they want to become and most especially what God wants to do with their lives. Many graduates are out of the university but still are living less of the standard of excellence because they lack vision for the future. Many businessmen in the workplace and entrepreneurs in the world of business never emerge for a lack of foresight and purpose. When vision is in view in any aspect of life, it drives the vision bearer to go all out to get the best quality and to become the best. Jack Ma who happens to be the richest man in China as at this writing, has created an excellent brand that started out in his small sitting room many years ago. He was able to achieve that level of excellence in his personal life and business because he envisioned this to be where he was going long before he was anywhere near it. He would tell his first staffs that their competitors were the biggest shots in the United States of America even while they were not yet recognized in their home town in China.

- **Vision brings about excellent initiative and innovations**

Henry Ford was able to invent an excellent car model that was simple, reliable and very affordable for all men whether rich or poor. When Ford envisioned this, it was a crazy thought because there was no method in existence that could make this possible. But by reason of his passion for the vision, the ideas and resources came. He was able to invent the assembly line machinery that made mass production tenable and attainable. He succeeded in accomplishing this because of his vision to make the best vehicles at the most affordable prices in a time when the economy was not friendly. Soon enough his vision became a reality such that automobile came within the economic reach of every man regardless of societal status. That was his vision and it was so clear. That vision was propelled by a passion. This enabled him to come up with an excellent way to produce a vast number of his car model at the cheapest rate possible. In the process he introduced to all manufacturers the method of mass production and that has affected the way things are done in the manufacturing sector forever. Vision for excellence brings about initiative. With the initiative, you end up developing new ways of doing something which others never even contemplated. When you possess a vision for excellence, it produces in you the professionalism required to climb up the ladder of greatness even faster and easier.

Getting the Best Jobs and Contracts by the Currency of Vision

- **Do not allow the society to decide your career path**

We cannot talk about getting the best jobs and contracts without clearly defining the place of vision in choosing a career path to follow. Jesus was twelve when he knew exactly what business and career path to follow. We may say "that was Jesus, He was the Son of God!" Well the good news is that if you are a born again kingdom citizen, you are a son of God and can also know what path God wants you to take in career or in business. A lot of people are confused in life because they find it difficult to identify what exact job, business or career they are uniquely suited for in life. Hence they do not know where to go or what to invest their time in. Some allow the pressures from society, friends and even family to decide for them. This is very important because even after graduating from high school with a degree in a particular course, you would still need to decide what exactly you want. You need to decide what path you want to take and you must not allow yourself to be boxed in by the opinions of people. Most students with great potentials find it difficult to choose a career path before they put in for their first degrees. This happens mostly to those who gain admission at ages ranging from 16 to 20 years. At this age a lot of them are not yet sure what areas they want to make their careers or if they want to eventually become entrepreneurs. If you are a young reader of this book and you are yet to make a career decision or about to choose a course of study, do not rush into making a decision. Before you make any choices try to learn about what the career field you are considering entails. Also research on its opportunities and disadvantages by asking questions from people who are already engaged in that field as professionals.

Some graduates do not know where exactly to go or where to work because their disciplines are so broad. For example, an individual with a degree in Chemical Engineering can fit into so many different career paths. He could pursue a career in food and beverages, pharmaceuticals, cosmetics, plastic, steel, military, paint manufacture, cement manufacture, oil and gas, research and development and a host of other different career paths. But one could have a degree in

Chemical Engineering and yet be confused as to which path to take. That is why you must be careful to discover yourself in order to make this choice. You do not need to wait till you graduate before becoming clear on that. You can devote time to discover yourself before, during or after your first academic degree. Even if you are a graduate in a particular discipline already, it is still never too late to choose the career path that you feel best suited for. There are several things to look out for when choosing a career path. First you must ask God for direction and guidance; tell Him to show you His plan for your life in the area of business or career. Then ask yourself "If I was not going to be paid, what kind of work would I still enjoy doing despite not getting a pay for it? **You need to find out what kind of work you really love to do for the benefit of people and can afford to do for free. But remember, what you can do for free can also be done for a fee with proper branding.** The job or business that is suited for you is going to be something that you do so well that when you do it, you get the most appreciation from others who benefit from it. The career that you are best suited for is the one that engages that talent of yours which has brought for you most of your successes and happiness in life. **Make your joy your job as long as it is a legitimate practice or service that adds value to humanity.**

Another clue to knowing what suits you for a job, career or business is that it engages skills that you learnt with ease and can do easily. It is something which a whole lot of other people find difficult and may even hate to do because of the discipline, diligence and dedication involved. Others who are not suited for it call it stress but you find it fun to engage in. It is also something that catches your attention. You love to think, talk and read about it. It attracts you just the way a banana fruit attracts a monkey. It is a job or business which you can work on for long periods without eating, or sleeping for long hours because you are absorbed in it whenever you do it. You admire and respect other people who are excelling in that endeavour, you want to be like them, be around them and learn from them. The moment you discover that thing that matches these descriptions, go for it whether it is a career or business. It actually makes no difference whether it is a career, a craft, an art, a business, etc. No matter what it is you can commit your life to it and watch your visions in that field come into a reality.

- **Is writing and submitting job applications unnecessary?**

Apart from the fact that millions of graduates are unemployed on a national and global scale, there are many others who are under-employed. This is because they have been forced by circumstances to settle for a job which they were not really cut out for just because they have not been able to get their dream jobs. They decided to settle for anything since nothing was forthcoming. That is why this book is a must read for students, graduates, businessmen and all others who want to experience the best that God has for them in life. When I say you can get the best jobs without an application, I do not mean that writing applications is not necessary. I only intend to communicate a higher way of doing things and getting the best results based on the word of God. That means that this book and the contents herein are not in any way trying to prevent people from writing application letters for jobs where necessary. It is only showing a more excellent way to get the best jobs by taking a hold of our kingdom inheritance, provision and principles. There is actually a more excellent way by which you can clinch the biggest deals, contracts and jobs without lobbying or applying. Mind you, there is absolutely nothing wrong with filing an application for a job opening. There are many folks who have received their big breaks because they applied for a vacant spot and got selected for a good job based on merit or whatever factor the employer deemed necessary for selection. That being said, there is a quicker and less cumbersome way to get your dream job.

According to research, there are some facts about the job search process that gives one an idea of what factors affect the rate at which job seekers get the jobs they so desire. This research is an eye opener to why many remain unemployed for a very long time. In this statistical study done in 2012, it was discovered that there were 3.6 million job openings by the end of that year. The painful truth is that about 80% of available jobs that year were never advertised. **That means the vacancies at the best spots in companies are hardly ever made public.** It was also discovered that out of the average number of people who apply for any given job, only 20% of those applicants get an interview.

Another sad truth about writing applications for vacant spots is that many companies use computer applications known as talent-management softwares to screen resumés. This is because most times, going through thousands of application letters, CVs and resumés is a very tedious process. Hence the computer software is used to knock out up to 50% of applications before anyone ever looks at a resume, cover letter or an application[5]. This contributes to why a lot of competent job seekers are still unemployed despite that they have submitted their applications to many establishments.

- How did Joseph get that top-notch appointment without application?

The story of Joseph is a typical case study which exemplifies how the currency of vision can furnish an individual with the best appointments, jobs and contracts, without even bidding or applying for them. When Joseph was a teenager, at the age of seventeen, he had seen a clear picture of his future. He really did not know exactly how that vision would come to pass but yet Joseph dared to believe in his dreams. Below is the account of Joseph's teen life.

Joseph, A YOUNG MAN OF SEVENTEEN, was tending the flocks with his brothers... JOSEPH HAD A DREAM, and when he told it to his brothers, they hated him all the more. He said to them, "LISTEN TO THIS DREAM I HAD: WE WERE BINDING SHEAVES OF GRAIN OUT IN THE FIELD WHEN SUDDENLY MY SHEAF ROSE AND STOOD UPRIGHT, WHILE YOUR SHEAVES GATHERED AROUND MINE AND BOWED DOWN TO IT." HIS BROTHERS SAID TO HIM, "DO YOU INTEND TO REIGN OVER US? WILL YOU ACTUALLY RULE US?" And they hated him all the more because of his dream and what he had said. Then he had another dream, and he told it to his brothers. "LISTEN," HE SAID, "I HAD ANOTHER DREAM, AND THIS TIME THE SUN AND MOON AND ELEVEN STARS WERE BOWING DOWN TO ME." WHEN HE TOLD HIS FATHER AS WELL AS HIS BROTHERS, HIS FATHER REBUKED HIM AND SAID, "WHAT IS THIS DREAM YOU HAD? WILL YOUR MOTHER AND I AND YOUR BROTHERS ACTUALLY COME AND BOW DOWN TO THE GROUND BEFORE YOU?" His brothers were jealous of him, but his father kept the matter in mind.

Gen 37:3-10 NIV

Joseph had a dream, and this dream was his vision for a

bright future. He knew there was a big picture which he would feature in and that it was only a matter of time before his visions became an actual reality. When Joseph had this dream, he believed in this dream so much that he began to tell other people about it. Eventually, he told his brothers about the dream and got into their bad books for having such a brilliant vision. They were intimidated by the enormity of his visions not knowing that Joseph's vision was actually standing upon the bedrock of God ordained purpose. ***Any vision that is not consistent with the purposes of God for you as an individual is not an authentic one.*** Now Joseph was in a strange country as a slave with no mother, father, friend, or connections whatsoever, but yet held onto his visions. He continues to walk in excellence, performing the duties given him in Potiphar's house with excellence and diligence. Before long, Joseph gets the best job as the manager of all of Potiphar's servants. A job promotion he never really applied for but got by reason of his exceptional abilities to manage things under his care. Soon enough, his master's wife begins to take note of Joseph for his dexterity and excellence on the jobs that he managed. But unfortunately, she has a seductive admiration for Joseph. She approaches Joseph with intentions of wooing him to bed with her but Joseph is too focused on his vision. ***Vision instills restraint and discipline on the visionary.*** Potiphar's wife feels embarrassed by Joseph's lofty personal values which were inspired by his great vision. She sets Joseph up and now the young man finds himself in prison. This seems like a demotion to Joseph, something far from what he had always envisioned as God's vision for his life. But Joseph remains undeterred. He keeps adding value to his immediate environment until the keeper of the prison notices him for his exceptional qualities. Joseph is now promoted even in prison but he still does not lose focus of his vision, he knows he does not belong to the prison regardless of the position he is handling there. He continues to sharpen his gifts and develop his skills. He also pays attention to the other prisoners to see how he can add value to them and one day he notices two of the prisoners who were looking sad. He spotted a need right there and helped them solve their problem of understanding their dreams, a skill he had discovered when he was a teenager. Now Joseph interprets their dreams and tells them to remember him when they get any similar contracts. And this is how he set himself up for a recommendation. Even though the men forgot to recommend him to the king immediately, when there was a need for the gifts which Joseph had always used as a blessing to people everywhere he went, the king's cupbearer remembered Joseph. That was the beginning of Joseph's turnaround story. Joseph was able not only to interpret the king's dream, but also proposed a solution for the problem he spotted.

"And now let Pharaoh look for a discerning and wise man and put him in charge of the land of Egypt. Let Pharaoh appoint commissioners over the land to take a fifth of the harvest of Egypt during the seven years of abundance. They should collect all the food of these good years that are coming and store up the grain under the authority of Pharaoh, to be kept in the cities for food. This food should be held in reserve for the country, to be used during the seven years of famine that will come upon Egypt, so that the country may not be ruined by the famine." The plan seemed good to Pharaoh and to all his officials. So Pharaoh asked them, "Can we find anyone like this man, one in whom is the spirit of God?" Then Pharaoh said to Joseph, "Since God has made all this known to you, there is no one so discerning and wise as you. YOU SHALL BE IN

CHARGE OF MY PALACE, AND ALL MY PEOPLE ARE TO SUBMIT TO YOUR ORDERS. ONLY WITH RESPECT TO THE THRONE WILL I BE GREATER THAN YOU." SO PHARAOH SAID TO JOSEPH, "I HEREBY PUT YOU IN CHARGE OF THE WHOLE LAND OF EGYPT."

Gen 41:33-41 NIV

Lessons from Joseph's Story

There are a few tips that one can pick from Joseph's story which landed him the best job in Egypt without an application. They are:

- Stay true to your core values; do not mortgage your values for immediate promotion or enticing offers. That means any job offer or contract that requires you to compromise your core values and virtues is not worth accepting. Had Joseph gone to bed with Potiphar's wife, he may have gotten some extra job incentives but would have lost his bearing in the process. If he had not gone to the prison, he would never have met the king's cupbearer and Egypt would have been swallowed up in famine. That means his family in Israel would also have been consumed by hunger in the process as there would be no Egypt to buy from (Gen 39:7-12).

- When you deliver a service or meet people to whom you have offered valuable service, try to always leave your contact information with them and get theirs. You never know where it may come in handy. Help others but leave them with your complimentary card or a means by which they could contact you when you are being recommended for the excellent services you once provided them (Gen 40:12-14).

- Here is the most important part. Learn to construct proposals channeled toward proffering solutions to problems. Always be ready to propose solutions to problems. Never dwell solely on the problems you spot in any environment you find yourself. As you diagnose problems always deliver solutions alongside. When Joseph diagnosed the problem by interpreting the king's dream, he did not stop there, he proposed a way forward. That was what gave Joseph the best job in Egypt without any application. When he did, Pharaoh looked for a way to keep him close. He had to create a new office and portfolio which never existed in his cabinet for Joseph (Gen 41:33-41). *I pray for you, that you would get that dream job offer you have desired as you begin to use these kingdom currencies. For your sake, new offices and portfolios would be created; even new companies would be built, just the way a new industry and portfolio was created for Joseph in Egypt in Jesus name!*

Building a Global Business Brand with the Currency of Vision

It cost nothing to use your imagination

If you want to build a global business brand that would touch lives and add value to the benefactors of the business, you must think generationally. You must be willing to identify the needs you are meeting at the present moment and how your solution to those needs can be integrated and built into the future. That is, you must be able to factor the future into your plans in such a way that your business would not become outdated as development and technological advancement kicks in. That is why vision is very important. It is only with the currency of vision you can meet a need that would last for hundreds of years after you are long gone. Everyone who followed God and allowed the visions of God for them possess them ended up becoming a generational figure, with a generationally relevant enterprise. The problem is that people are too scared to think big, dream big or to imagine greatness. It is needful to remind you at this point that it cost absolutely nothing to use your imagination. Using your imagination is all about holding images of what you can see of your future in your mind for long periods of time. Do not let the fear of any obstacles or of your present financial circumstance limit your imagination. Just use it, after all, you lose nothing when you put your mind to use, and stand a greater chance of achieving everything your mind can envision or imagine by the inspiration of God.

The Lord said to Abram after Lot had parted from him, LIFT UP YOUR EYES FROM WHERE YOU ARE AND LOOK NORTH AND SOUTH, EAST AND WEST. ALL THE LAND THAT YOU SEE I WILL GIVE TO YOU AND YOUR OFFSPRING FOREVER. I will make your offspring like the dust of the earth, so that if anyone could count the dust, then your offspring could be counted. Go, walk through the length and breadth of the land, for I am giving it to you.

Gen 13:14-17 NIV

Notice what God told Abraham, "All the land that you see, I will give it to you and your offspring forever". God was using Abraham's vision to determine how much Abraham would get and enjoy. If Abraham did not use his mind at that moment to picture the world, he would never have experienced the wealth which he is famed for.

There was a man who had a childhood full of extreme challenges on his mind. As a child, he was tormented with hallucinations and blinding flashes of light in an excessive manner. He failed to complete his university education and had to leave his job due to a nervous breakdown. He then decided to take control of his wild imaginations and hallucinations by reason of a vision for a brighter future. He started directing his hallucinations towards creating his own imaginary world. He started inventing new machines with his imagination. He would develop a device in his mind and model it completely in his imagination. He would even remodel it and upgrade the features where necessary. This man would even go as far as test running the device in his mind without sketching or working the formulas out with pen and paper. He sort of creates a laboratory in his mind and uses his powerful mind to check the innovation for any form of strain or disorder. After doing all these in his mind, he then goes ahead to turn the vision he had in his mind, which was just an idea, into a reality. When this is done, a new device is innovated. This man gained global relevance with his extraordinary vision, perception and imagination. His name is Nikola Tesla. He became one of the greatest inventors and patented over 278 inventions in 26 countries around the world minus those others that were not patented.[5, 6] He developed inventions which became global brands through the power of vision and imagination.

Take advantage of the mentoring principle

Mentoring plays a very powerful role in helping the mentee, student or apprentice, master and cultivate excellence in an art, trade or in life generally. Mentoring is the art of guiding, instructing, training and coaching a person in a field or endeavor where the mentor has a certain level of expertise. Mentoring has little or nothing to do with age as the mentor could be older or younger than the student, mentee, apprentice or protégé. It is a learning and development relationship between someone with vast experience and someone who wants to learn. King Uzziah was a teenager when the mantle of leadership fell on his shoulders. He had no choice but to lead, but he had a coach who the Bible records had understanding in the visions of God. The name of his mentor was Zechariah and this man did a great job as King Uzziah's coach. This is easy to deduce because the Bible records that Uzziah prospered by reason of Zechariah's coaching and mentoring.

SIXTEEN YEARS OLD WAS UZZIAH WHEN HE BEGAN TO REIGN, and he reigned fifty and two years in Jerusalem. His mother's name also was Jecoliah of Jerusalem. And he did that which was right in the sight of the Lord, according to all that his father Amaziah did. AND HE SOUGHT GOD IN THE DAYS OF ZECHARIAH, WHO HAD UNDERSTANDING IN THE VISIONS OF GOD: AND AS LONG AS HE SOUGHT THE LORD, GOD MADE HIM TO PROSPER. And he went forth and warred against the Philistines, and brake down the wall of Gath, and the wall of Jabneh, and the wall of Ashdod, and built cities about Ashdod, and among the Philistines. And God helped him against the Philistines, and against the Arabians that dwelt in Gur-baal, and the Mehunims. And the Ammonites gave gifts to Uzziah: AND HIS NAME

SPREAD ABROAD EVEN TO THE ENTERING IN OF EGYPT; for he strengthened himself exceedingly.

2 Chron 26:3-8 KJV

One of the primary objectives of true mentors is that they help broaden your horizon and bring more clarity to your vision on a very close and personal level. Mentorship is most effective when there is one on one working relationship between mentor and mentee. This was what the teen king enjoyed and it was as though a sixty year old king was on the throne. King Uzziah stood on the shoulder of Zechariah, gaining support from him as one who had understanding of the visions of God. King Uzziah became a threat to other nations because of the innovations he brought into the way he engaged in battle. The Bible declares that his name spread abroad meaning he became a king with regional influence by reason of Zechariah's mentoring in the visions of God. Many businesses fail because of the lack of mentors.

As at the time of this writing, one of the world's top ten youngest billionaires is the co-founder of the biggest social media platform on planet earth. His name is Mark Zuckerberg, the co-founder of Facebook. This young chap is known to have become so great by virtue of the influence of his mentors among whom was Bill Gates, co-founder of Microsoft, Steve Jobs, co-founder of Apple Inc., Don Graham, former Chairman of Washington Post, Marc Andreesen, and others. A lot of people always wondered how this young chap became so intelligent, that he was able to create a global business brand which made him a billionaire at 23 years of age. The answer is obvious; he was smart enough to get into a mentoring relationship with great men despite his very tender age. That helped him think globally and avoid some pitfalls on the road to making Facebook become a global business brand.

Ensure to give adequate supervision to your vision

Another thing about vision is that it requires high level excellence to replicate vision and to reproduce it in physical terms. Have you ever desired to make a dress with a particular fashion style in mind? Did you give the task to a dressmaker mandating him to produce the same style you envisioned for the fabric? How did you feel when the dressmaker gave you something different from the style you instructed him to make? I am sure you were disappointed. Every visionary who desires to build a global business brand and a successful one at that must be ready to pay attention to details. Sometimes when you have a vision, you would require determination and excellence to bring it into fruition. Most times, it takes the Spirit of Excellence to reproduce the images of your mind in physical and tangible equivalents.

... I WAS NOT DISOBEDIENT TO THE VISION from heaven.
Acts 26:19 NIV

In order to build a global brand, you must not deviate from the vision you had when you were in the conception phase. During the construction of Disney Park, Walt Disney made sure all the different details were represented properly on paper and on site. If Walt Disney did not like what his studio designers came up with, he would go ahead and do it himself. Tom Sawyers Island was a typical example of this. When the plans were presented to him, he thought his designers had misunderstood and misrepresented the idea. So Walt took home the plans and the next day he designed it exactly the way he envisioned it to be. The way it appears today is exactly how Walt designed it. Now Disney World is known to be one of the most visited vacation resort in the world.

Make this tabernacle and all its furnishings EXACTLY LIKE THE PATTERN I WILL SHOW YOU. SEE THAT YOU MAKE THEM ACCORDING TO THE PATTERN shown you on the mountain.

Ex 25:9, 40 NIV

It is one thing for you to have a vision but a totally different thing to be able to develop the vision excellently according to the model and pattern of the vision. That was why when God gave Moses the vision of building Him a tabernacle He emphasized the need for everything to be excellent. God stated that everything must be built according to pattern. In other words, God was telling Moses to pay attention to all the details in order to reproduce it excellently in physical form.

There are situations where you cannot get the highest level of excellence due to some possible limiting factors like availability of resources but regardless of that, you can still achieve excellence based on whatever resources you have. Excellence does not come by abundance of resources; excellence can be cultivated at any level of provision that is available to you per time.

- **Let the business be driven by a desire to empower your staffs and clients.**

Henry Ford had a vision to build a horseless carriage. This man came from a poor background and was uneducated. He chose not to wait for opportunity to favour him but to create his own opportunity by working with the tools he had. He said to himself "I will build a motor car for the great multitude. It will be so low in price that every man will be able to own one." While most other automobile manufacturers were building luxurious automobiles for the wealthy, Ford had a different vision, for which he was classified as crazy. His dream was to create and develop automobiles that everyone could afford. Ford accomplished this vision because he was out to add value to everyone. He captured everyone in society when he envisioned his automobiles being in use. He made automobile that was very affordable for the masses and that sparked a revolution. He was the one who introduced mass production into the world because of his vision to make it possible for every home to have a car owner and to satisfy the enormous demand he got for his product. Henry Ford brought the pleasures of owning and riding the automobile to as many people as possible, and also provided a large number of high-paying jobs in the process. He became so wealthy by reason of that drive which spurred up a great ripple effect in the global business chain.

Keys for Converting the Currency of Vision into Tangible Wealth

Develop and share your vision statement.

Vision entails having in your mind's eye, a clear picture of your God ordained future as though it is already a present moment reality. After developing a vision statement for yourself, business or career it is advisable that you share it with someone who would give you the needed support that you require. Many people are afraid to share their visions and hence miss opportunities when they come. If you share your vision with the right people, you stand a chance of finding the people who may want to help you bring it into fruition.

I and some business associates chartered a vehicle to take us on a trip from Benin City to Akure, Ondo State for some business development. On our way back we got into a conversation with the cab driver who chauffeured us. As the conversation progressed I discovered that the cab driver was a graduate. He was an educated man who lost his job when one of the Oil companies decided to lay off some workers. He spoke intelligently and seemed to me to be full of prospects. When I discovered this, I wanted to get him connected to somebody influential who I knew would be willing to help such an enterprising young man. So as the conversation went on I asked him, "What is your vision for life, career and business?" To my greatest bewilderment, this man turned down my question. He said his vision was personal to him and that he would never share it with anybody. I was surprised at his naivety. This man almost missed out on that golden opportunity because he failed to share his visions with me on that trip. I had to persuade him for long telling him that if he keeps his vision to himself, he would never be able to find the people who God has destined to help him turn his vision into reality. He finally opened up and shared his vision with apologies after he discovered who I was and how that I could actually help him achieve his visions. You must be very sensitive to find people who may be interested in knowing your visions. They may be the ones to introduce you to friends, acquaintances and colleagues who could help you. They could even supply you with resources you require to make your ideas into tangible equivalents. To share your vision does not necessarily mean you are asking for anything from the person. Just sharing it alone would go a long way to release all the invisible forces needed to bring the vision to pass. Sharing it is an indication that you believe in your visions and when that is in place no devil can steal your destiny from your hands.

Set God inspired goals.

Many people have wonderful visions that may never become a reality because they do not have God inspired goals. There is a difference between a vision and a goal. They are not the same thing, even though they can both work well together. Goal setting is important because it turns aspirations into tangible objects by stirring the goal setter towards commitment and action. One thing goal setting does for you is that it helps you overcome procrastination. The habit of procrastination is one of the biggest weaknesses of the human nature. Like a popular saying goes, procrastination is the thief of now. How true! Postponing what can be done today into a time in the future severely reduces one's chances of making progress. However, if you have a set goal for yourself, you would always be on the move and you would find yourself doing what is required to achieve those goals. Imagine a football game without a goal post, what would it be like? It would be a meaningless toil for twenty two young men to run around a pitch with nothing to motivate their movements and decisions. Goal setting will make you become more productive and cause you to take a more direct route to the accomplishment of the goal. You would accomplish your visions in good time and waste less energy engaging in fruitless activities when you set God inspired goals. You would become more deliberate with your efforts without running around in circles.

Brothers, I do not consider that I have made it my own. But one thing I do: forgetting what lies behind and straining forward to what lies ahead, I PRESS ON TOWARD THE GOAL for the prize of the upward call of God in Christ Jesus.

Phil 3:13-14 ESV
Paul in the above verse speaks of how he was able to make consistent progress in his ministry. He tells us how he deliberately refused to dwell too much on his past and kept on an onward march toward his calling and vision. His goals kept him focused on daily improvements despite his successes and setbacks. Without goals, a person may be tempted to rest on his oars when there is more to be accomplished ahead. You could also be forced to allow setbacks discourage you if you have no goals. But when you set God inspired goals it produces an irrepressible urge to accomplish great things. This urge acts as a propellant driving you toward activities that would bring about the attainment of your goals; especially when the goals are set appropriately.

Whenever I set goals for myself in the morning concerning what I want to accomplish for that day, I discover that an unusual force carries me through that day in such an amazing manner. That is what properly set goals do. It makes you experience an upsurge in your energy levels. You would become more passion driven and would gain control of your life. This is so because the fact that you have set goals communicates to all your body cells that you know where you are going and intend to take the necessary steps to get there. And because you are the captain of the ship of your life, your crew members, which include all the cells of your body, begin to move in the direction of the set sail. Your life would at such points, no longer be left to chance or fate because you create your destiny and accomplish your visions with your goals.

Learn to sell your visions at every opportunity

A lot of people do not really know what selling is all about. Most people think selling only takes place when they take some products to the market square and offer it up for sale. Selling does not only involve the act of transferring goods or services in exchange for money. It also involves promoting a person, an idea, a viewpoint or an option over another. **When you present an idea before people with the aim to influence or persuade them to co-operate with you, choose something over another, or to take a particular course or direction, you are selling.** If you must be a successful person in any field you are involved in, then you must understand the science and the art of selling. Dr. Martin Luther King Junior is a typical example of a man who sold his dreams most effectively and he did so at every chance he got. He sold his vision to the whites and the blacks of his day in his famous "I have a dream" speech. At first when he communicated his vision to the American populace comprising of both whites and blacks, the whites did not buy into his vision because it sounded like a farce, an idiotic drama. But the blacks gradually bought the idea and the revolution began.

When America's first black president, Barrack Obama stood on the steps of the Lincoln Memorial on Wednesday, August 28, 2013, the reality of Dr. King's vision statement of fifty years ago was reborn in a more tangible form than ever before. It was the 50th anniversary of the Martin Luther King's "I have a dream" speech. History played out the power of vision that remarkable day. It was no coincidence at all that the same place Dr. King delivered his "I have a dream" speech on August 28, 1963, happened to be the same place former USA president, Barrack Obama stood to deliver his speech. That a black president was standing there to deliver a keynote in memory of Dr. King's speech was a tangible proof of what looked like a figment of the imagination 50 years earlier. It had become a more visible reality for the black race and for the world at large to see. In his speech, Mr Obama acknowledged the strides made since Dr King's time, when segregation was still the norm across the southern United States and when civil rights demonstrations were met with police resistance[8]. These strides would never have been made had Dr. King kept his dreams to himself and never shared it.

Dr. Martin Luther King's vision still echoes in the heart of every American political leader today because he sold his vision for a new nation to the populace and they were able to buy into it and run with it. *If you would become great, you must have a vision for greatness and sell it to people even when you look like nothing near great*. Many people may laugh at you, some may not even take you seriously, but soon enough, when the visions begin to take visible form, they would be the ones to tell others the story. When you sell something, it is no longer yours because you have traded it in exchange for something you need. There are those who sell their visions cheaply just for immediate gain. There are also others who sell their visions so adequately that the returns from the sales of their vision reproduces the reality of the vision that was sold as just an idea. When this happens vision is transmuted and converted into tremendous and tangible equivalents.

Be focused on your vision.

Focus brings productivity and productivity generates income. Even athletes know that vision can only get one to the tracks, but to win the race, it takes focus. When you focus most of your time and energy on the development of your vision, you are able to bring out the best of yourself and your potentials. Many people lose focus as they try to embark on the journey toward vision accomplishment. They tend to be distracted by other people's opinions of their visions and begin to pursue different things at a time. If you want to achieve results that are extremely phenomenal and derive complete satisfaction in your life's work, business, career, or project, you would need to get focused on your vision. When talking about focus, it really is about taking a hold of your daily activities and channeling all your efforts towards things that would drift you closer to the accomplishment of your vision. To get this kind of laser beam focus, you need to be crystal clear on what your visions are. You have to be resolute and definite about where exactly you want to go. People who are focused on their visions are in control of their life. They do not live by chance or allow life and its challenges to control them. Even in the event where some situations happen to be beyond their control, their responses and reactions to such events are easily controlled and handled based on the preconceived vision. Some people give too much attention to the past, and as they do, they lose their present and apparently mortgage their future.

The light of the body is the eye: IF THEREFORE THINE EYE BE SINGLE, thy whole body shall be full of light.

Matt 6:22 KJV

The Bible in the verse above talks about the eye being single. The word eye is used as a metaphor to refer to "the eyes of the mind". The word "single" on the other hand, comes from the Hebrew word that means to be "fulfilling ones office". By reason of this, it is therefore clear that the scripture above was speaking particularly about focus. The moment the eyes of the mind are singled and focused, it has a resultant effect on the whole body of the individual and regulates his actions.

Having a clear and thoroughly clarified vision and focusing on it does something tremendous to the vision bearer. It causes a sudden change in your lifestyle, behavior and even habits. It gives you the traction you need to exert discipline on yourself and take daily actions that would culminate in extraordinary outcomes of productivity. If you must convert your visions into provisions, then you must prioritize your vision and allow your vision influence your life only in positive measures. You must regulate your use of time, what you put your money into, the opportunities you accept, and even the relationships you keep. When you focus on your vision, decision making process becomes a bit easier to go through because your decisions would be guided by the visions you hold in your heart.

See your visions as already accomplished.

Vision helps you see not just what is, but also what can be and gives you the opportunity to make plans that would guide you steadily and gradually to your destination. In the book "The Principles and Power of Vision", Myles Munroe shares a very wonderful story about Walt Disney which in no small way buttresses this point. He stated how one day, Walt Disney was sitting on a bench and staring into thin air. Disney world had just opened and had only one ride. One of his workers, who was dressing and tending the grass, came past him and said to him, "How are you sir?" Without looking at the man, he said, "Fine", and kept on staring. So the man said, "Mr Disney, what are you doing?" and he responded, "I'm looking at my mountain". "I see a mountain right there." Mr Disney not only saw the mountain as though it was already completed, he went ahead to share the vision he had with his architects about this mountain. As he talked, they took note of what he said and then they drew up the plans. Unfortunately though, Walt eventually died before Space

Mountain was built, hence he never witnessed its construction. But because he already charted his course and plotted the graph of where he wanted his business to be and the need he would be serving, his death made no difference. His business was as though it was on autopilot. When Space Mountain was finally dedicated, the governor and the mayor were at the ceremony, and Walt's widow was also there. One of the young men stood up to introduce her and said, "It's a pity that Mr. Walt Disney is not here today to see this mountain, but we're glad his wife is here." When Mrs. Disney walked up to the podium, she looked at the crowd, and said, "I must correct this young man. Walt already saw the mountain; it is you who is just seeing it".[9] Walt had already charted the course of his mega business which eventually became a global brand and still remains a phenomenon till date. This was possible because he saw his visions as already accomplished even when he had nothing to show for it.

The word of the Lord came to me: "What do you see, Jeremiah?" "I see the branch of an almond tree," I replied. The Lord said to me, "YOU HAVE SEEN CORRECTLY, FOR I AM WATCHING TO SEE THAT MY WORD IS FULFILLED."

Jer 1:11-12 NIV

When God speaks to you, or brings an idea into your heart, you must be able to see the ideas and visions in graphic pictures. When you see your visions in pictures as though they were already accomplished, you release the power of God into action to bring the vision into reality.

Develop a plan for the short term, medium term and long term.

To turn vision to reality, there must be a laid down action plan for its accomplishment. That action plan must capture the vision in such a way that would make it actionable and achievable. This is the part where a lot of people find some difficulty. Everyone can dream big but not everyone is willing to take action. Some take action with no plan for the distant future and not so distant future. Every business must have a growth plan. Growth must be the goal of all business activities. You must also have a profit growth plan that is as detailed as possible. In order to develop this profit growth plan, your question should be, "How do I add more value to my customers? How do I get my customers to become clients? How do I get more customers? How do I get referrals from my customers? How do I satisfy my customers better?" If you sit yourself down, take a piece of paper and brainstorm along these lines by writing the answers that come to your mind. You will be amazed the ideas that would be brought to your mind. These ideas would give you better ways to add value through your business brand. You should have a growth plan for the number of prospects you intend to reach and for the number of new customers you intend to attract from those prospects. Everyone who wants to build a global business brand must have a plan for short, medium and long terms if he intends to do well. Failure to have a growth plan would lead to starvation and stagnation of the business. Growth is not an accidental occurrence. It comes by definite, deliberate and intentional planning. If you want to build a global business brand you must have mapped out a well articulated growth plan. Most times individuals only think and plan for their growth in the beginning of a New Year when a lot of people are making all sorts of New Year resolutions. But appraising yourself in the beginning of a new year is not enough. You must be able to narrow your plans and resolutions into short term goals that can be measured by certain benchmarks.

SUPPOSE ONE OF YOU WANTS TO BUILD A TOWER. WILL HE NOT FIRST SIT DOWN AND ESTIMATE THE COST TO SEE IF HE HAS ENOUGH MONEY TO COMPLETE IT? For if he lays the foundation and is not able to finish it, everyone who sees it will ridicule him, saying, 'This fellow began to build and was not able to finish.'
Luke 14:28-30 NIV

Jesus Christ was teaching His disciples the power of planning before developing a project. He makes it easy to understand that before you can truly build a global business brand or convert vision to provision, you must plan. A lot of people get into a job with absolutely no plan for growth. Some are living in the self deception that they have job security and retirement benefits and they spend about 35 years of their lives going to a job without adding value to themselves. They feel secure in the fact that when they retire, they would have a gratuity to fall back on. Many pensioners die of high blood pressure, heart attack and frustration when they discover that their pension cannot cater for their needs as they expected. At this point in their lives, it is most of the times, too late for them to begin to rediscover themselves.

Communicate the vision effectively to your team.

Imagine what would have become of his vision if Walt Disney never communicated it to his wife, architect and other team members. He would have taken the pictures of a great empire with him to the grave leaving everyone with no clue as to what should be done. He believed his visions would become a reality and it did because he told others about it. He communicated it properly to his team members and that brought about the reality of his vision. No one can achieve excellence without defining for himself what he would accept as excellent. And more so, no one can reach the mark of excellence without the support and contributions of others. No one can truly get the best jobs without seeing it first with the eyes of his mind. Even if he gets the best job by influence, connections or by chance, he would lose it because whatever is too big for the mind to capture would be too much for the hands to nurture. Vision is an excellent and ideal picture of the future. No one can build a global business brand all by himself without a team of people who believe in his vision and are willing to go all the way to see it accomplished.

Then the Lord said to me, "Write my answer plainly on tablets, so that a runner can carry the correct message to others. THIS VISION IS FOR A FUTURE TIME. IT DESCRIBES THE END, AND IT WILL BE FULFILLED. IF IT SEEMS SLOW IN COMING, WAIT PATIENTLY, FOR IT WILL SURELY TAKE PLACE. IT WILL NOT BE DELAYED.
Hab 2:2-4 NLT

Every true vision is generational in time perspective and hence outlasts the visionary. The founder of McDonalds is gone but the business is still growing. The fonder of Disney World is gone but the business name is still pulling its weight in the business world. No one ever achieved any extraordinary feat without the currency of vision. Every great accomplishment that the world ever witnessed was realized because somebody or a group of people had a vision, a mission and a purpose.

CHARGE

If you desire to achieve excellence, you must envision it first and see yourself walking in excellence by the Spirit of God. The same principle holds if you desire to get the best jobs without going through the struggles associated with applying for one. You must be able to picture the ideal job you want, and imagine that all the obstacles and constraints that would ordinarily have pulled you back do not exist. The moment you can do this and hold that picture long enough, you would see that your life would begin to align with your visions. See your business the way you want it to be in the near future now. Then begin to take steps that are in consonance with bringing your business to the level of your visions.

AFFIRMATIONS

Thank you Father because your thoughts toward me are thoughts of peace and prosperity. You have given me a bright future and now I know that my end is definitely better and more glorious than the beginning. My mind is focused on achieving greatness because God has destined me for greatness. I refuse to be moved by the circumstances surrounding me right now. I choose to lift up my eyes above any limitation around me. I call forth the men, materials, resources, finances and every provision I need from the vast store of the kingdom central bank. All I see is increase, provision, abundance prosperity and wealth. I will not fail nor be discouraged. I am patient and consistent with accomplishing my God inspired goals and visions. Thank you because all things are working together for my good, to bring my visions into manifestation. I am blessed beyond measure because my visions are coming to pass. They are being converted into tangible realities by the grace of God. Thank you Father, for I am blessed in Jesus name!

FOOD FOR THOUGHT

Purpose beggars the question "why am I here?" while vision triggers the question "where am I going?"

- What you need in order to start developing your vision into a global brand is to think big, plan big, but start small right from where you are.

- It is better to start small and grow big than to start big and grow small.

- You need to find out what kind of work you really love to do for the benefit of people and can afford to do for free.

- Whatever you can do for free can also be done for a fee with proper branding.

- Any vision that is not consistent with the purposes of God for you as an individual is not an authentic one.

-

CHAPTER THREE
THE CURRENCY OF
DILIGENCE

"Diligence is the mother of good fortune, and idleness, its opposite, never brought a man to the goal of any of his best wishes".

Miguel de Cervantes-Spanish poet

We live in a world full of billions of talented people who never truly achieve greatness because they lack the diligence required to get to the level of excellence that is needed to go higher in life. Nothing in the world can take the place of diligence. Not even talent can take the place of diligence. Most unsuccessful men are talented people who failed to diligently polish and harness their gifts and talents. Thomas Edison's quote remains one of the greatest of all times on the topic of diligence, persistence, hard work and dedication. He said that genius is a product of 1 percent inspiration and 99 percent perspiration. Another profound authority on the subject of diligence is Orison Swett Marden. This man who was one of the earliest bestselling authors of the 1890s in America said, "Show me a really great triumph that is not the reward of persistence. Genius, when you look more closely at it, usually turns out to be the sum of uncommon dedication to a task". What would make a man try something 1,000 times and keep at it despite all the failed attempts until he discovers what he wants? Only a priceless currency known as diligence can do that.

What is Diligence?

According to Samuel Johnson, "few things are impossible to diligence and skill; great works are performed not by strength, but by persistence." When someone displays constant and earnest effort to accomplish a task at hand, diligence is said to be at work in that individual. Most people tend to think that diligence only means hard work. But the truth is that there is a lot more to diligence than only hard work. A person can be hard working with the wrong techniques, skills and methods. That cannot be described as diligence because that person is engaged in a tedious and unproductive task for a lack of wisdom and skill. An individual could struggle, toil and labour rigorously for years on a task or job for which he is ill-suited. But when you take that same person and put him in the right field or give him the right method to work with you would be amazed at his level of productivity. The word diligence connotes a show of determination to achieve something either by developing the required know-how, skill and, or by being consistent in attempting to accomplish a given task with best practice. Diligence produces not only hard work but also smart work. It impresses upon individuals the right attitude towards work and it helps people cultivate proper work ethics. Diligence can also be understood as persistent action and continuous development in the direction of a goal, mission or vision until it is accomplished. Diligence is what makes a man fail at an endeavour and not merely give up, but keep trying again in a more intelligent and determined way until he gets the desired result. It is careful and persistent effort in pursuing a defined goal. According to Orison Swett Marden, there are two basic qualities required for success. He called the first the "get-to-it-iveness", and the second the "stick-to-it-iveness". I want to say these two qualities summarize the word diligence in a most succinct manner. This is because diligence is more about one's ability to get to work when such a person does not feel like it. Diligence is also the ability to stick to a given goal and its accomplishment even when everyone else shies away from the responsibilities that come with achieving it.

Seest thou a man DILIGENT IN HIS BUSINESS? he shall stand before kings; he shall not stand before mean men.

Prov 22:29 KJV

Michael Jordan is known to be one of the greatest basketball players of all time. When Michael Jordan was young, he loved to play basketball so much. His earnest goal and desire was to be able to play in competitive events. Every day he and his brother who was taller than him competed in a one on one intense match and usually his brother dominated him. Somehow, the high school coach came to know Michael through his brother Larry and got Michael invited to the basketball summer camp. This was prior to Michael's enrollment into high school. Michael was given the opportunity, along with a close friend of his, to try to qualify for the university team group. At the summer camp, everyone admired Michael's speed and skill, but the coach did not pick him for the team at the end because of his height. When the list of names of the university team was released, Michael did not find his name on the list. However, his mates, all of who were 198 cm in height were selected. He wept as he stared at the list of alphabetically arranged names feeling almost sure that his coach had left his name out by mistake. When he got home, his mother came to his side, comforted him and inspired him with some important words that instilled in Michael the "stick-to-it-iveness" he needed to become one of the greatest basketball legend of all times. She told him that the best thing he could do was to prove to the coach that he had made a mistake. Michael ran off with those words and began to work even more diligently to sharpen his skills and improve his performance. Michael Jordan rejoined the university's junior team. He got so much better that he was recognized as a dedicated player but he did not rest on his oars, he increased his training intensity. Soon enough, Michael's sport instructor noticed a change in his practicing regime. He trained so diligently, persistently and consistently in autumn, in winter, in summer, all year round. Most times his instructor would have to ask him to leave the court before he would stop training due to his dedication.

Diligence is an attribute which when possessed, causes one to continually work toward his goals or a given task while making use of available resources and opportunities. Diligence is also what makes one vigilant to avoid errors and to stay focused on the task at hand. Diligence does not rely on talent. Talent is cheap; the world is full of millions of talented people who die with their talents because they lack the commitment, industry, and perseverance to transform their talents into a global business brand.

Though Michael Jordan's height was still a challenge being under 183 cm, through his diligence and practice regime he soon became a favourite player in the junior team of his university. He had developed such speed and skill that his team mates were no match for him. Before long, the university team players started to come earlier to the games just to watch how Michael led the junior team to victory. Sometimes he would score 25 to 40 points in a single game. Michael instilled the same discipline on his teammates and pushed them to develop into a true team by demanding diligence and intensity of training from his team mates as he did to himself. Soon enough, Michael's height increased by 10 cm. He also developed large hands with the advantage of catching and holding the ball better and then was also able to do slam dunks. His coach was delighted to see the changes in Michael's height that he just could no longer neglect his skill and talent. Michael eventually got into the university team and brought something different and unique into the team. This uniqueness was diligently cultivated and that was one of the things about him that inspired every coach, team mate and fan throughout his career. His life was not a rosy life of talent but it was a life that preached the message of diligence so loudly. He made it clear through his life experiences that everyone and anyone can achieve an unparalleled and unrivaled level of skill through diligence, dedication, consistency and commitment. Another lesson to draw from his story is to always appreciate failure and refuse to be deterred by disappointments. Rather one should use setbacks and failures as stepping stones to greater heights of success. Stick to your dreams and visions despite the setbacks that may come your way. Take advantage of it in a way that you would produce goodness out of such bad experiences. Maybe you were denied visa to further your education, do not be discouraged but rather use that as a motivation to push harder in other possible places where you can get the same kind of education. That experience made an indelible impact on Michael throughout his career. Whenever he achieved some measure of success and felt like slowing down to relax he could not fall for the trap of complacency. At such moments he would close his eyes and see again the list that didn't include his name at the beginning of his career and immediately that memory came, his spirit was revived to continue improving himself.

Diligence as a Kingdom Currency

According to Investopedia, a hard currency is a currency that is widely accepted around the world as a form of payment for goods and services [1]. The currency of diligence can be likened to a hard currency in this respect because no matter where you go on earth, diligence is always recognized, rewarded and appreciated. No one can deny the currency of diligence when it is at work, especially when it has been converted into fruitful and tangible results. The value of diligence in any endeavour cannot be overemphasized and must not be underemphasized. Diligence is a hard currency which many people wish they could do without on the road to destiny fulfillment. Everyone who fulfilled the purposes of God for their lives in scripture did so by being diligent at what they were called to do regardless of the challenges they encountered. The Bible is abundantly clear about the fact that diligence produces wealth. Solomon spoke a lot about this currency called diligence and most of the time he expressed diligence as a prerequisite for exceptional accomplishments.

He becometh poor that dealeth with a slack hand: but THE HAND OF THE DILIGENT MAKETH RICH.
Prov 10:4

To be slack means to be inconsistent and lax, to move or respond slowly with a lack of zeal, eagerness and enthusiasm with regards to work. Dealing with a slack hand is what produces procrastination and laxity. It also refers to one who does not have an energetic and dutiful attitude towards his business. He responds to his career or business with no motivation or eagerness. He acts and works as though nothing is at stake even when he knows otherwise. He has an "I don't care attitude" towards his business. The Bible says such a man would become poor as long as he deals and engages in his work with a slack hand. Many students deal with slack hands in their academics. They resume a semester two to four weeks after the actual date of resumption. Some others resume early but wait till it is one month or two weeks to the examination before they begin to study their books. They believe nothing is at stake as long as they can cram their textbooks a few days to the exam and at least avoid having to flunk a course. They are cool with an average performance as long as they do not fail out rightly. That is the beginning of mediocrity and that is why poverty always catches up with the one who deals with a slack hand. The hand of the diligent is well able to produce excellence, hence wealth is never far for a diligent person.

Achieving Excellence by the Currency of Diligence

- **Be dedicated to accomplishing your visions.**

Michael Jordan said one time, "in order to excel, you must be completely dedicated to your chosen sport". How true! In much the same way, if you want to achieve excellence in the "sport" called academics, you must also be completely dedicated to your chosen course of study. Many students have raw hidden talent in them but have not been able to tap into it because they have not been able to render due diligence to attending class, or paying attention in class, or studying and, or researching on their fields of study. If you want to excel in a given business, you must be completely dedicated to making it grow. The reason why many businesses go under is partly because of improper management. Many people start up businesses that never succeed as a brand because they are unwilling to dedicate the time which may be required to make it blossom.

Seest thou a man DILIGENT IN HIS BUSINESS? he shall stand before kings; he shall not stand before mean men.

Prov 22:29 KJV

One of the founding fathers of the United States of America, who was among those who drafted America's Declaration of Independence Act, goes by the name Benjamin Franklin. Dr. Franklin experienced the reality of the above scripture firsthand. He only had two years of formal education but educated himself through diligent and passionate reading, personal study and research. He was an industrious man who became known as a Diplomat, inventor, writer and a scientist. His scientific accomplishments included investigations into electricity, mathematics and even mapmaking. He invented bifocal glasses and structured the first successful American lending library known as the Library Company of Philadelphia[2]. According to Benjamin Franklin, he set apart an hour or two each day for study. With that he was able to make up for his lack of formal education. Reading was the only thing that delighted him and that was his only luxury. He refused to spend any time in taverns, games, or on any kind of frolics. He was an industrious businessman. One of his father's frequent instructions to him when he was a boy came from a lesson in the book of Proverb which says "Seest thou a man diligent in his calling? He shall stand before kings; he shall not stand before ordinary men". This instruction instilled in Franklin, the attitude of diligence and industry. By reason of that, Franklin saw diligence as a means of obtaining wealth and distinction, and that encouraged him to develop a very strong work ethics. Whenever Franklin's father would admonish him on the virtue of diligence and the benefits that follow, he would listen to his father's counsel. That notwithstanding, Franklin never really thought he would ever literally stand before kings through diligence the way Proverb 22:29 put it. But as God would have it, he actually had several hobnobs with royalty at different points in his life's walk. Benjamin Franklin stood before five kings, and even had the honor of sitting down with one to dinner[3]. He met with George II and George III of England, Louis XV and Louis XVI of France, Emperor Joseph of Austria, and then got the rare honour of having dinner with the King of Denmark. Today, his face is in the United States of America's hundred dollar bill, making him one of the most respected men in the United States of America.

Getting the Best Jobs by the Currency of Diligence

- **Whatever you do, do it with all your might.**

God has given us the capacity to utilize the currency of diligence in our daily lives because His might and ability is at work in us. You have no idea how far you can go when sponsored by the currency of diligence. Being diligent does not necessarily mean you have to be a jack of all trade. It does not also mean you should invest your time, energy and resources on just anything that you see others doing. But you must be able to identify an area where you have passion and drive so that diligence becomes natural to you. When you are engaged in work which you have passion for, diligence is automatic and its results are mind blowing. There is a place for desire and passion if the currency of diligence needs to be invested in something. No matter what you are passionate about, whatever it may be, ensure that you are diligent in your approach to it and the results that would follow will amaze you.

WHATEVER YOUR HAND FINDS TO DO, DO IT WITH ALL YOUR MIGHT, *for in the grave, where you are going, there is neither working nor planning nor knowledge nor wisdom.*

Eccl 9:10 NIV

Where pedigree, talent, certificates, formal education, earthly currencies and influence may be lacking, the currency of diligence could make up for you. For example, Joseph had a vision to be a great man. When he was sold as a slave in Potiphar's house, he did not allow that stop him. He displayed exceptional work ethics and that caused his master to entrust the upkeep of the whole house to Joseph. He made Joseph overseer of all the other slaves because he was skilful and diligent. He made himself to be sought for by diligently honing his skill.

A very accomplished man who at this writing was the Vice President of the Federal Republic of Nigeria, Professor Yemi Osinbajo, shared a story on his Twitter handle. The story was about a man who surprised him with a wonderful car gift one day in the early months of 2017. In that tweet, the vice president went down memory lane and narrated a very touching story. He shared on how he was a young lecturer then at the Department of Law, University of Lagos, Lagos State. During his time there, he required the services of the departmental typists to get his academic materials typed since laptops and personal computers were not common in the country as at that time. According to his narration, there were three typists – the chief typist, the senior typist, and the junior typist. The Vice President who was a Professor of Law and also happened to be an ordained pastor in one of the biggest congregations in Nigeria observed the attitude of these three typists towards work. Two of the three had very poor work ethics, but one of them who had the lowest level of qualification known as school certificate qualification was the most hardworking of them all. According to his post he said, "When there was work to do, what I discovered was that the chief typist would disappear. He works only till 4 p.m. The senior typist would be nowhere to be found. But the gentleman, Adereni, the junior typist, who only had his school certificate, was remarkably diligent. Sometimes I would drop him off at his home at 1 a.m.," Prof. Osinbajo said. Several years later, the Professor began to work as an adviser to the then Attorney General of Nigeria, Hon. Bola Ajibola. Interestingly enough, Hon. Bola Ajibola later became a judge of the World Court at The Hague in the Netherlands. One day, Hon. Bola Ajibola called the Professor and asked if he could recommend a good secretary who was hard working and could do long judgments. Professor Osinbajo in this dramatic story recalled the scenario in a very revealing manner. He said in that tweet, "I had three options, the chief typist, the senior or the junior typist. The junior typist at a time had only school certificate, he didn't have any other qualification but I chose him". Can you imagine that? Having the rare privilege to work alongside an honourable judge of a globally recognized court at The Hague in Netherlands, with an ordinary school certificate and a meager salary? That is both incredible and remarkable. In the words of the Vice President, "He got to The Hague, and typically worked hard and diligently. Every judge in the court wanted him to work with them. He later moved his family over to The Hague and got degrees and made a good living for himself"[4]. Without a high profile certificate, he got a top notch job in a high profile institution where he never even dreamed of submitting a application because of his work ethics.

Building a Global Business Brand with the Currency of Diligence

- **Think like the best and work like the best**

People who end up taking over a particular market, or blazing the trail in business have something in common. They think like the best and work themselves toward becoming the best even when they are yet unpopular. Before you know it, their businesses have taken over the markets, the charts and the media. No business success happens overnight. It comes by reason of cumulative acts of diligence. Once upon a time, there was a young Chinese boy who was not a particularly good student. He was lousy at math and failed a test two times before he could even get accepted into what he later described as the "worst university" in his home city. At a very young and tender age, however, he discovered that he had fallen in love with the English language and wanted to be fluent at it no matter the cost. By sheer determination, he began to practice the language by riding on a bicycle for 40 minutes to a hotel where he could have opportunities to engage in dialogue with foreigners and tourist travelers. He was eventually accepted into a university where he studied to become an English teacher. When this young Chinese boy graduated, he was the only one out of 500 students that had the singular privilege and honour to be assigned as a teacher at a university. He had planned that when he finished doing five years as a teacher, he would join a business. He was determined to go out there and do something worthwhile. In the year 1995, he managed to travel to the United States and this was when he got exposed to Internet for the first time. Immediately this young man was introduced to the internet, he spotted a big vacuum in the web because as an international trader, he had discovered that when investors and foreign traders come to China to source for manufacturers because of their cheap labour, they always encountered difficulty due to the language barrier. This inspired him to establish a company known as Alibaba.

In 1999 when he was addressing his employees on the vision and mission of his company, he said, "Our competitors are not in China, but in America's Silicon Valley... We need to learn the hardworking spirit of Silicon Valley." In order to achieve that vision, this Chinese entrepreneur marketed his business like a global brand, and he never ran away from contending with market competitors that had more money or more fame. At this writing, this man had become the richest man in China. He is also known to be among the world's 50 richest men. This man rose up the ladder of wealth from a small village in the south eastern part of China and built a global business brand by virtue of diligence. He is a true reflection of the fact that diligence pays. Even though he grew up poor during the communist era of China, failed the entrance exam into university twice, and was rejected from countless jobs, including one at KFC, he was determined to succeed. His determination brought upon him the diligence that he needed to run a successful business. Through diligence, he found success with his third internet company known as Alibaba[5].

Keys for Converting Diligence Currency into Tangible Wealth

Determine never to be idle

If you are a kingdom citizen, you have the currency of diligence. But you need to be decisive and determined to put that diligence in you into action. Make a resolve never to be idle any time and any day no matter what the condition of your day looks like. You can even take ownership of some idle moments like when you are driving to work by listening to educative tapes, inspiring messages and audio books. Even when you are on transit from one place to the other in a train or a public bus, you can read an eBook on your phones and electronic devices. While waiting for your plane to arrive in an airport or while traversing the planet on the plane, you can do some work on your laptops or tablets as long as you have the energy and alertness to do so. Dr. Myles Munroe was a renowned professional speaker who normally got about 800 invitations to speak to audiences in different parts of the world per year. Despite his busy travelling schedule, he was able to write more than 50 books in his lifetime and read at least 48 books every year. He accomplished this by taking advantage of idle moments spent in the airport when his flight is delayed or times spent being chauffeured through a long distance. He would pick up his laptop and start working on a book he was writing while waiting for his delayed flight to be cleared. On other occasions, he would pick up a book and read while on transit. This man maximized the currency of diligence and took advantage of it in a phenomenal way. No wonder he was so full of wisdom and was able to write so many books while on a hectic travelling schedule as a public speaker. In maximizing the currency of diligence, you must watch out for people who are idle themselves and are looking for other people who they can also pull into the state of idleness. Paul the Apostle warned his son Timothy against such people in the verse below.

BESIDES, THEY GET INTO THE HABIT OF BEING IDLE AND GOING ABOUT FROM HOUSE TO HOUSE. *And not only do they become idlers, but also gossips and busybodies, saying things they ought not to.*
1 Tim 5:13 NIV

There are a lot of gossips and busybodies everywhere including the house of God. You have to be careful not to allow them get your attention otherwise you would be amazed at how you would become addicted to idling about. I remember an old proverb that says "an idle man is the devil's workshop". When you allow idleness to take a hold of you, you become unproductive and begin to poke nose into other people's affairs. You would begin to go from place to place engaging people in idle chit chat. You would not be able to think of businesses you can do to help meet a need in the society nor would you be able to give your best at work. This is a very dangerous place for any kingdom citizen to be.

Laziness casts one into a deep sleep, and AN IDLE PERSON

WILL SUFFER HUNGER.

Prov 19:15 NKJV

Refuse to be a lazy person:

Golden opportunities hold no value before a lazy person, but a diligent and industrious man is one who can make the commonest opportunities appear golden. Everyone has his field where he possesses a competitive edge. Doing your best to achieve your goals in your particular field of calling is what diligence is all about. But the sad truth is that there are many gifted people who lack the currency of diligence and hence are lazy. The lazy man dreams of easy money without any effort. A lazy person is very good when it comes to dreaming big and unrealistic dreams. But his dreams are always unrealistic because they are not followed up by hard work. the lazy man believes he is going to win the lottery or win it big with a ponzi scheme. He plans to get rich quick without any structures on ground to produce the wealth. This kind of attitude is what breeds tricksters, thieves and robbers who try to rip people off their hard earned money at every opportunity. The book of Proverb has a lot to say concerning lazy people. King Solomon apparently knew that laziness was a disease that needed serious attention. Here's what the Bible says about laziness:

How long will you slumber, O sluggard? When will you rise from your sleep? A LITTLE SLEEP, A LITTLE SLUMBER, A LITTLE FOLDING OF THE HANDS TO SLEEP - SO SHALL YOUR POVERTY COME ON YOU like a prowler, and your need like an armed man.

Prov 6:9-11 NKJV

Talent without diligence would never produce any result.

Jesus told an interesting parable that clearly shows us that having talent is never enough. There were three servants and each one of them was given talents according to their abilities. Two out of the three of them traded diligently with their talents. Because they combined their talents with diligence, they produce more talents. When you begin to develop the skills and talents you possess, you would begin to discover new skills and talents that you never had. That is what diligence does to talent, it refines and multiplies it. One of the three servants actually did nothing with his talent. That is the problem with lazy people. They are full of ideas and big visions but never do anything to make their talents add value to people. According to the parable, the one who did nothing with his talent but hid it was referred to as a lazy servant (Matt 25:14-30). Lazy people are also known as unprofitable people because they are unwilling to put in calculated efforts required to produce profit. Remember that the Bible says that in all labour there is profit (Prov 14:23).

WE WANT EACH OF YOU TO SHOW THIS SAME DILIGENCE TO THE VERY END, in order to make your hope sure. WE DO NOT WANT YOU TO BECOME LAZY, but to imitate those who through faith and patience inherit what has been promised.

Heb 6:11-12 NIV

According to the above verse, Paul makes it clear that diligence is required for anyone to be able to make his hopes sure. That means hopes, expectations, aspirations, dreams and visions remain unsure unless they are consolidated upon with diligence. Paul was very careful to ensure that the people he was writing to were diligent to the very end. Another attribute of laziness is to start something and not finish what you have started especially when you discover the tough work involved. Of course there are some kind of task that you are not built for. Even though you work night and day on such tasks, you would never achieve much because it is not within the range of your core competencies. But when you have identified your area of strength and yet fail to invest yourself diligently in it, you are being lazy. Paul's advice to us is not to be lazy. He encourages us rather to follow after those who have realized the promises of their visions and hopes through diligence, faith and patience.

Choose never to be a burden to anyone but a blessing

Even though I am a firm believer in the idea of rendering financial and material help and assistance to people when they are in need, I cringe when such folks tend to be complacent with a beggarly lifestyle. This attitude is demonstrated when someone chooses to rest on his oars because it seems like he has someone who wants to help him. There are a lot of people who take delight in begging others for handouts and are doing absolutely nothing on their own part, to change their financial status. The Bible teaches us not to take on that kind of attitude because it only tends to poverty. Apostle Paul displayed an exemplary lifestyle and taught the people of Thessalonica to work diligently so that they would never be a burden to people. The verses below show us one of his instructions in that direction.

For you yourselves know how you ought to follow us, FOR WE WERE NOT DISORDERLY AMONG YOU; NOR DID WE EAT ANYONE'S BREAD FREE OF CHARGE, BUT WORKED WITH LABOR AND TOIL NIGHT AND DAY, THAT WE MIGHT NOT BE A BURDEN TO ANY OF YOU, not because we do not have authority, but to make ourselves an example of how you should follow us.

2 Thess 3:7-9 NKJV

I know of a man who used to seek for handouts from people. He would always beg for money to buy food after church services. He would ask several different people and get handouts from most of these people on service days. For a while, it appeared to him that it was working and so he kept doing this. It now became a habit for him that everyone began to avoid him. When this man saw that he had become a renowned beggar all of a sudden, he remembered that he had hands to work. It dawned on him that those whom he begged were no better than him, so he decided to engage diligently in farming. As he did, God blessed the work of his hands and his farm began to yield a bountiful harvest. He became so prosperous that he began to employ others to farm for him. Before long he began to supply farm products to different markets and was making a huge turnover. This man quit begging because he saw that it was more honorable to work and be rewarded for your work than to beg for handouts. He began to have more than enough money to pay his bills and to give to others who were in need. What a turnaround! He ceased from being a burden to people who he always begged for bread money, and had now become a blessing to others. Your case may not require that you go to farm, but if you look inwards, everybody has something to offer for which people would gladly pay them. The moment you decide to put that gift to work no matter what age you are, you would become self sufficient.

Never be content with always receiving handouts from people even if they are your parents. Begin to think of things you can do to be financially free as soon as you can. You can always do better than being a dependant because everyone has the innate capacity to work and fend for himself at different degrees. Paul by virtue of his position as a great Apostle would have been able to depend on the church to feed him because of his influence but he did not do that because he did not want to overburden anyone with his personal issues. ***If you must seek help from others, ensure that you are not asking for bread but for seed.*** If you ask for bread today, there is a great chance that tomorrow and the day after that, you would keep begging for bread. But if you choose to ask for seeds, whether it is seed money or business capital, you are on your way out of dependency. This is because when you plant your seeds, in due season you would begin to harvest bread for food and seeds for further planting. That way you may not need to beg anyone again. But when you keep requesting for bread from people, chances are you would become a burden to them and they would begin to avoid you.

Refuse to make excuses for laziness and failure:

Be very careful not to blame others for your failures or to make excuses for whatever state you find yourself. Whenever you blame others for what happens in your life, you give the power to control your situation to others. Try to look for a positive interpretation of any situation or the actions of individuals if you can.

*The sluggard says, "There is a lion in the road, a fierce lion roaming the streets!" As a door turns on its hinges, so a sluggard turns on his bed. The sluggard buries his hand in the dish; he is too lazy to bring it back to his mouth. **THE SLUGGARD IS WISER IN HIS OWN EYES THAN SEVEN MEN WHO ANSWER DISCREETLY.***

Prov 26:13-16 NIV

I have come to discover that it takes an intelligent man to make excuses for laziness. That is why the scripture above tells us that the sluggard is wiser in his own eyes than seven wise men put together. How did the sluggard know that there was a fierce lion roaming the streets when he is still sleeping on his bed? Does it not amaze you? That sluggard must be super intelligent. He seems to have surveillance cameras on all the street buildings that must have given him a view of what was happening in the streets while in his bedroom. Or maybe he has informants around feeding him with falsehood just to help him justify his laziness. If this sluggard is so intelligent that he could manufacture intelligent excuses without much effort, I believe that same sluggard would accomplish so much if he chooses to think of ways to overcome excuses. A sluggard is always coming up with new excuses as to why he would not take advantage of opportunities even before stepping out to perform the tasks. Stop thinking of why you cannot do something that you know is critical to your progress. Rather channel that intelligence toward how to overcome the object of your excuse. If you know that there is traffic on the road that hinders you from resuming work early, instead of making that an excuse, channel that intelligence towards thinking of ways you can beat the traffic. *The difference between a lazy man and a diligent man is in the way they think. The lazy man invests his time, resources, energy and creativity digging out excuses and reasons why he cannot perform a task critical to his success and prosperity. But a diligent man channels all of his time, energy, resources and creativity towards finding a way around potential obstacles.* These are obstacles which the sluggard sees as a good enough excuse for his idleness and ultimate failure. That is why Solomon tells us that what distinguishes a diligent man for abundance and plenty is the way he thinks in his mind regarding potential obstacles.

THE THOUGHTS OF THE DILIGENT TEND ONLY TO PLENTEOUSNESS; but of every one that is hasty only to want.
Prov 21:5-6

This is interesting! One would have thought the distinguishing quality that separates the diligent man from the sluggard is their muscular build. But on the contrary, it is the way they see potentials in what looks like an obstacle or threat to their successes. Diligent people think about solutions rather than focus on problems with intentions to make excuses out of them. Do not think like a lazy man but like a diligent man. When you do, ideas of wealth and wealth itself would gravitate towards you.

Be Persistent no matter the circumstance.

There was an American bestselling author named Orison Swett Marden who was born into a poor background. During his college days, he worked as a caterer and also worked in hotel management. He was able to save up to $20,000 (USD) which he used as capital after his formal training. With that money he began to invest in business. He was able to establish a resort and he also bought a chain of hotels in Nebraska. In 1893, there was a serious depression in the United States of America and this affected Orison's businesses. He suffered repeated financial reversals during this depression and he lost his hotel as a result. At the time this happened, Orison who was forty four years of age, decided to switch career from being a business man to becoming a professional author. Despite the serious setbacks he had suffered in business, he decided to write a book that would motivate people and inspire them to persist despite the hardship and difficulty which the nation was facing at that time. Orison therefore went on to get a little room and began to write, he spent an entire year working night and day as he wrote a book he had titled "Pushing to the Front". When he finished his manuscript one day, he decided to go out to have dinner since he was very hungry. While he was away, his room was gutted with fire and the entire manuscript was in ashes. This manuscript which was over eight hundred pages had gone up in smoke and there was nothing left to recover from the fire.

Regardless of this setback, Orison out of sheer determination, persistence and diligence went and got a new notebook while his room was still in the smothering from the fire. Even though he was initially heartbroken, he picked up himself again and began to rewrite the manuscript from the memory of his dream book. After he finished rewriting the manuscript, he tried to get it into the hands of several publishers but none was interested in a motivational book. They thought such a book would not sell as people were in challenging financial times. Unemployment was very high and the depression seemed to be having the better part of the nation. When Orison moved to Chicago where he got another job, his friend introduced his work to a publisher friend. That was how this book "Pushing to the Front" got published and eventually became the single greatest runaway bestseller in the history of personal development books at that time. This book was so great that American politicians and presidents like William McKinley, Theodore Roosevelt, and even the Prime Minister of England, William Gladstone, praised the book. Respectable inventors and influencers like Henry Ford, Thomas Edison, Harvey Firestone and J. P. Morgan made references to this book as a major inspiration for their great accomplishments. This book would have forever been lost in the flames of the past but for his determination accompanied by persistent and diligent effort put in by the author to make the book a dream turned reality. Orison Swett Marden went on to write fifty or more books and booklets during his career. This man said, "The world makes way for the determined man. Everybody believes in the man who persists, sticks, hangs on, when others let go. Tenacity of purpose gives confidence". It takes diligence to possess the tenacity of purpose. Discovering purpose is not all that there is to achieving fulfillment but being tenacious in your pursuit of purpose is the key to accomplishment.

Be consistent.

One key factor that must be in place if you want to build a global business brand is consistency. Consistency is a necessity for any notable accomplishment. A lot of people are challenged in this area. No matter what field you have decided to be dedicated to, whether sports, academics, arts, entertainment or marketing, consistency cannot be overemphasized. It takes diligence to achieve that kind of consistency. Every great journey begins with a first step; however, if we must get to our final destination, we must be willing to take repeated next steps until we finally arrive to our ultimate goal. If you really look closely enough, most overnight successes took a long time to emerge. Consistent and repeated practice is what makes greatness in any field or endeavour.

Easy come, easy go, but STEADY DILIGENCE PAYS OFF.
Prov 13:11
A lot of people hate to follow through with this principle

because they want to emerge overnight. They want to cut corners in order to become wealthy at the expense of consistent practice and diligence. Wealth that comes through cutting corners never pays off on the long run. It cannot be sustained except you want to consistently engage in wrong practices and cut corners to stay wealthy and the truth remains that those are dangerous grounds to tread. True wealth comes through diligence in following through with God's principles for wealth. Taking repeated steps of diligence causes your wealth to grow. If your finances go up without God's principles of wealth, it would surely come down. But if it grows up through diligence, focus, determination, dedication and consistency in applying these principles, it would stay up for generations without end.

He becometh poor that dealeth with a slack hand: but THE HAND OF THE DILIGENT MAKETH RICH.

When I was writing the original manuscript for one of my books, I learned a lesson on diligence. I would tell myself that I would write when I get inspiration, but no inspiration would come after several days of waiting. I would always have a reason not to be inspired to work on my projects each day. It was either I was tired from the days' outing, or I was too busy with the day's activity to gain the "inspiration" which I needed to further work on my book project. As the days went by I discovered that if I actually waited until I received a special feeling to write in the name of "inspiration", I would never achieve my goals. I decided that I would write at least 2,000 words each day whether I had inspiration or not. I discovered that it was an excuse my mind was playing on me to cause me to deal with a slack hand. The moment I made that decision, I saw the hand of God enabling me. As I mandated myself to write with or without that "special feeling", I noticed that whenever I sat down to write, fresh ideas and inspiration would begin to open up to me. I discovered that most times, the inspiration comes after you have begun to put your hand to work. I began to receive great ideas that would never have come to me if I had not begun the task. No wonder Edison said that genius was 1% inspiration and 99% perspiration. Refuse to be slack in working towards your goals and visions because of one excuse or the other. Do not wait for situations to line up before you engage the currency of diligence, the world only makes way for a determined man. Just begin to move and work toward the direction of your vision and situations would line up as you take determined steps toward your goals.

Become a Specialist in a field of interest before diversifying.

Most people want to do everything all at once in the name of being diligent. Being diligent does not mean you should be busy exerting yourself in many different areas at the same time. When you do, your energy would be dissipated in many different directions with no tangible results. If you are into business, ensure you focus on one area and become effective and productive. When you have been able to establish yourself in that area as an authority, you can then diversify into other areas. The richest man in Africa, Alhaji Aliko Dangote, first of all established himself as an authority in the construction industry by specializing in the manufacture and distribution of cement. After gaining sufficient ground in that line of business, he diversified into salt, sugar, flour, beverages, pasta, steel and several other commodities. At this writing, he is said to have expanded further into the oil and gas sector[6]. He is setting up a $12 billion (USD) refinery in Lagos State, Nigeria to be completed in the year 2019. He intends to also supply 12,000 Megawatts of energy to Nigeria and neighboring countries through the refinery[7]. He applied this principle and because he had become a major player in the cement industry, it was easy to diversify into other areas.

Expanding your tentacles into other areas that may be of interest to you becomes much easier when you have mastered a particular discipline or field. This is so because the credibility and experience you would have obtained while thriving as a specialist would give you the edge as you spread into new areas. To be a specialist means to streamline one's focus to a specific area in your pursuit for education, business, career or ministry. This is done while maintaining a general grip of knowledge about other things. Those who succeed in any endeavour are known to always have one thing which they use to establish themselves as a brand, before moving unto other areas. They always specialize in an area related to their business, ministry, career or life's purpose. They never fall victim to the deception that acquiring knowledge is supposed to stop after going through school. When they decide to go to school for further studies, they do so with a specific area of knowledge in view and know the purpose for choosing whatever they decide to study. That is a very important point to note for one who intends to go further especially in academic pursuit. If you decide to go for additional formal education, you must first ascertain the purpose for which you desire to receive the knowledge you intend to acquire.

Do not waste time on frivolities during working hours.

Many people are not productive at work not because they are unskilled or not good enough to deliver high end results. On the contrary, they do not get results because they never truly maximize their work hours. They hardly ever complete their tasks because they are not diligent with their working hours. By the time you take out public holidays, sick leaves, lunch breaks, and lateness to work coupled with several other times spent absent from work, the hours of work left is greatly reduced. By reason of these and some other factors, the average person works for about 30 hours a week. In those 30 hours which they spend at work, a lot of people waste 40 percent of the time operating their phones, chatting with friends, roaming about the office, reading newspapers, surfing the net and hanging around social media platforms like Facebook, Instagram, Snapchat and the likes. By the time you do the math, you would discover that these people who claim to be working in an office are actually not working. They engage in frivolities during working hours and wonder why they are still struggling to survive the inflation and economic meltdown in their earthly nation.

When I was in the university, a lot of students were victims of this. They were seen to put in so much time in their studies but get so little. They go to reading classes and spend five hours there. The first 30 minutes is spent browsing on Facebook, the next 15 minutes on Instagram, and then they begin to reply all the chats on their instant messaging platforms for the next 15 minutes without knowing. Their first one hour in their reading classes would have been spent on frivolities. They begin to read and in the next two hours, they answer every call that comes into their phones. Then they look at the time and discover they have spent 3 hours sitting in their reading spot forgetting that the first hour which is the most productive was spent on Facebook without actually "facing their books". They then decide to take a stroll down the block to say "hi" to a friend on the fourth hour. By the time they are done, another hour is gone. They spend the fifth hour back on their books struggling to focus on the books because their minds have been subjected to heavy distractions. After some time, they decide to go back to their hostels with their books. When their roommates see them returning from the reading class, they begin to praise them for spending five hours reading, not knowing that it was only about two out of the five hours that was actually spent reading. When such a student performs averagely or a little below average in the semester exam, everybody is surprised. They are wondering what happened because they think that student was always going to read for long hours. They do not know that the student always spent 60 percent of those "reading hours" on frivolities.

In some countries where people are paid by the hour you would hardly find that kind of attitude. This is because they know the implication of every hour on their income and cannot afford to waste a minute of their time on frivolities. They are able to track their wages and have the full understanding that they are the sole determiners of how much they get paid. If you come around such people during their work hours to engage in irrelevant chats, they would either ignore you or be prepared to lose their wage for that hour in exchange for idle chats.

Approach your work or discipline with the attitude that you get paid by the hour and you would see how effective you would become. Imagine that you get paid handsomely on an hourly basis for your work. What would you do with your time and how would you spend your work hours? What if you are being watched throughout work time by a superior to see that you do the work you were being paid for, would you answer every phone call and roam about the office? What if your boss placed a webcam in your office to monitor you, would you spend your working hours browsing all the social media outlets? This is one of the best ways you can control your negative work habits and avoid wasting precious work time.

Listen diligently to the voice of God.

God established David as a brand in his days because he would not take any decision without consulting Him. He was known to never lose a battle because he would always inquire from God before going into any battle. If you would fulfill your destiny in a grand style, you must learn to be someone who listens to the voice of God. I have come to discover that listening to the voice of the Spirit takes commitment. It takes commitment to heed the counsel of the Lord and to actually carry out the instructions which He tells you. God taught the Israelites this principle when they were in the wilderness. By reason of that, they understood the place of diligence in being led by God. It takes diligence to obey the instructions of God because we live in a world where there are many voices clamoring for our attention.

"NOW IT SHALL COME TO PASS, IF YOU DILIGENTLY OBEY THE VOICE OF THE LORD your God, to observe carefully all His commandments which I command you today, that the Lord your God will set you high above all nations of the earth. And all these blessings shall come upon you and overtake you, because you obey the voice of the Lord your God: "Blessed shall you be in the city, and blessed shall you be in the country. "Blessed shall be the fruit of your body, the produce of your ground and the increase of your herds, the increase of your cattle and the offspring of your flocks. "Blessed shall be your basket and your kneading bowl. "Blessed shall you be when you come in, and blessed shall you be when you go out. "The Lord will cause your

enemies who rise against you to be defeated before your face; they shall come out against you one way and flee before you seven ways. THE LORD WILL COMMAND THE BLESSING ON YOU IN YOUR STOREHOUSES AND IN ALL TO WHICH YOU SET YOUR HAND, and He will bless you in the land which the Lord your God is giving you.

Deut 28:1-8 NKJV

When you are a diligent listener to the voice of God, you save yourself the effort that would have been wasted on trial and error approach to things. Many people are working hard with no results to show for it because they are not diligent in the place of seeking and taking direction from God. When you diligently hearken to God's instructions, you would be more effective because you would know exactly what to do and when to do it. You would know exactly what career to pursue and what business to venture into. It pays to listen to God before you engage in any task because God rewards only those who diligently seek him. That means that it is not working hard in an arbitrary way that produces wealth. Rather it is when you work in the direction of God's guidance that your effort and diligence would be rewarded.

Master a skill, art, science or trade through diligent practice:

Anything that you practice regularly and from time to time eventually becomes habitual. The truth about life is that no notable improvement and progress takes place overnight. Even though we live in a fast world where everyone wants to get immediate rewards and overnight perfection, the reality remains that becoming a master at anything takes diligent practice. It takes investment of time to gain mastery at anything, even when you seem to have natural talents and gifts, you would need to hone your skill through constant practice. As you get involved with an art, skill, trade or any endeavour and you maintain constant and daily practice on that thing, you begin to gain mastery in it. Even the Bible states that maturity in the things of God comes by training and constant practice.

But solid food is for the MATURE, FOR THOSE WHO HAVE THEIR POWERS OF DISCERNMENT TRAINED BY CONSTANT PRACTICE to distinguish good from evil.
Heb 5:14 ESV

It takes years of study, training, practice and research to gather experience, gain the length, breadth and depth of knowledge and to master different scenarios in your field of passion and gifting. But without the currency of diligence, you may never be able to endure training. It took Moses 40 years in the wilderness with herds of sheep to master the art of leading a mammoth crowd of people with different personalities and temperaments. Yours may not take such protracted number of years but it sure would take some time invested in diligent practice depending on what needs to be accomplished. We live in a world where people expect to become masters without ever being an apprentice or mentee. We live in an age where many want to acquire knowledge without study. David was not such a man to fall prey to that trap. He was to go against an accomplished warrior who had so much charisma and had scared off the trained military men in King Saul's army. David was given the rare honour to wear the king's armour and to brandish the king's sword. Who would not want to handle the best sword in Israel's artillery? But David understood the value of mastery through diligent practice. He rejected that golden opportunity to use a weapon he had never trained with regardless of how prestigious it would have been and he chose to stick to his sling because he had mastered the art and science of using a sling. He would rather be ridiculed for using a sling which he had mastered than take up a weapon he had not trained and learned how to handle. The story has it that David with one shot from his sling, left Goliath helpless on the floor and left the Philistine army with no choice but to flee. Had he gone to that duel with Saul's charismatic armour and special sword, the anointing notwithstanding, he would have been ground to powder.

Saul put his battle tunic on David; he put a bronze helmet on David's head and dressed him in armor. DAVID FASTENED SAUL'S SWORD OVER HIS CLOTHES AND TRIED TO WALK, BUT HE HAD NEVER PRACTICED DOING THIS. "I CAN'T WALK IN THESE THINGS," DAVID TOLD SAUL. "I'VE NEVER HAD ANY PRACTICE DOING THIS." SO DAVID TOOK ALL THOSE THINGS OFF. He took his stick with him, picked out five smooth stones from the riverbed, and put them in his shepherd's bag. With a sling in his hand, he approached the Philistine.

1 Sam 17:38-40 GWT

Notice David's statement, "I have never had any practice doing this". He went on and selected five smooth stones because he had mastered its use by practice. It was only a matter of taking one determined shot at Goliath's head and the giant was dead. Even God requires that we practice diligently thereby using this hard currency called diligence. The truth is that David's display of skill and accuracy was a result of his diligent practice. Natural talent, gift or anointing would never undermine the place of diligence in achieving greatness. Anointing speaks louder when diligent practice and preparation is in place.

The more you are perceived by others to be a master in an art or an expert in a particular discipline, the more admiration you would get. By reason of David's display of mastery and the result that followed, he got much admiration, reputation and recognition.

When the men were returning home after David had killed the Philistine, the women came out from all the towns of Israel to meet King Saul with singing and dancing, with joyful songs and with tambourines and lutes. As they danced, they sang: "Saul has slain his thousands, and David his tens of thousands."

1 Sam 18:6-7 NIV

This was a shepherd boy who was not really regarded by his family because he was the last child. The women of Israel who came to welcome the soldiers from the battle where the Philistines were defeated admired him and sang songs to appreciate his value. **The better you become at your chosen discipline whether as a student, an academician, an engineer, a trader or a farmer, the more you would gain the attention of the key people in your field who can bring you promotion and recognition.** The more you also come into the attention of other experts in your field and more doors would be opened unto you.

Ask for more Responsibility at your office when you feel underutilized.

Brian Tracy is one of the most successful sales coach and public speakers in the United States of America at this writing. Worthy of notice is the fact that this renowned professional speaker is also a devoted believer and follower of Christ. He has consulted for more than one thousand companies and addressed more than 5 million people in 5,000 talks and seminars throughout the US, Canada and 70 other countries worldwide. As a Keynote speaker and seminar leader, he addresses more than 250,000 people each year. This wonderful thought leader, who has also authored over 70 books at this writing, shared a very enlightening story in his book titled "Goals". He wrote about a piece of advice which he oftentimes offers when he addresses business students of any graduating class in the corporate world of work. Whenever he gets the chance, he tells them, "as soon as you get settled in at your new job and you are on top of your work, go to your boss and tell him or her that you want more responsibility". He encouraged them to make affirmations to their bosses on how that they are determined to make the maximum contribution possible in the organization and that they would like more responsibility whenever it becomes available. He also told a personal story of how he tried it when he was a young executive in a large corporation. This company had about 200 employees and he was one of the lowest ranks. He was stuck in a tiny office space at the back with just a desk, a chair and no picture frames on the wall. He was only given a variety of small tasks to work on and the tasks varied from one week to the other. After a few weeks of this boring and unexciting experience, Brian was a little frustrated. He therefore went to his boss, who was the Chairman of the company, and told him that he was already on top of his work, and that he wanted more responsibility. When he approached his boss with this daring request, his boss accepted the request but did nothing particular about it. That notwithstanding, he kept reminding him from time to time.

After a few weeks, his boss gave him a project to study and evaluate and according to Brian Tracy, he jumped at it. He worked diligently on it and submitted his report in record time. In a week's time another task was given him by his boss outside his normal duties, which he did diligently and submitted long before the deadline. Before long, more tasks began to come to him on account of his diligent approach to new challenges at work until one day he gave him a responsibility. And as usual, Brian acted swiftly on it without any delay. On this particular task, Brian had to fly a thousand miles, working day and night to get the job done. Because of his swift response to the responsibility, Brian discovered a fraud and saved his company from losing $2 million (USD). After that, heavy doors of finances flung open to him. In two years of working for the company, he was moved into the second largest office in the building. In addition to that he began to handle three divisions within his corporation involving about $50 million (USD) worth of transactions and managing a 50 member staff from these three offices. His coworkers who were still operating below their full capacity and doing their ordinary regular duties with ample time for luxury began to call him "lucky". They thought their boss was being unfair to them, not knowing that the currency of diligence was what set Brian Tracy apart from them all. It may sound like asking for too much or biting more than you can chew, but this is far from that. You as a person must access your threshold to know if you are performing below capacity or not. If you discover you have extra capacity which can be channeled towards more, then why waste your time doing nothing with your extra capacity?

David said to Saul, "Let no one lose heart on account of this Philistine; your servant will go and fight him." Saul replied, "YOU ARE NOT ABLE TO GO OUT AGAINST THIS PHILISTINE AND FIGHT HIM; YOU ARE ONLY A BOY, AND HE HAS BEEN A FIGHTING MAN FROM HIS YOUTH." BUT DAVID SAID TO SAUL, "YOUR SERVANT HAS BEEN KEEPING HIS FATHER'S SHEEP. WHEN A LION OR A BEAR CAME AND CARRIED OFF A SHEEP FROM THE FLOCK, I WENT AFTER IT, STRUCK IT AND RESCUED THE SHEEP FROM ITS MOUTH. WHEN IT TURNED ON ME, I SEIZED IT BY ITS HAIR, STRUCK IT AND KILLED IT. YOUR SERVANT HAS KILLED BOTH THE LION AND THE BEAR; THIS UNCIRCUMCISED PHILISTINE WILL BE LIKE ONE OF THEM, BECAUSE HE HAS DEFIED THE ARMIES OF THE LIVING GOD. The Lord who delivered me from the paw of the lion and the paw of the bear will deliver me from the hand of this Philistine." Saul said to David, "Go, and the Lord be with you."*

1 Sam 17:32-37 NIV

This principle was exactly what David applied to get to the top of his career with such speed. David understood his capacity. He knew he could do more than just tending his father's flock in the bush. He wanted more action and responsibility. From serving his brothers food at the war front, he became Saul's personal bodyguard without necessarily applying for that spot. When David was sent by his father to take food to his brothers in the battle front something happened. These trained soldiers had been arrayed in battle with the Philistine army only for them to stage their best man Goliath in a one on one duel with whoever was man enough to take the challenge. While his brothers and the entire army command including their overall boss, King Saul, shied away from taking responsibility for the challenge. David stood up and said, "I am tired of being a shepherd boy guarding flocks of sheep in the fields, I want more responsibilities sir!" When King Saul questioned his credibility, David pulled out his résumé and showed Saul how his capacity was being underutilized. He told Saul how he had killed a bear and a lion with bare hands. And that was how Saul added more responsibility to David and gave him the task of taking on the "Goliath project". David eventually delivered on that project in a most surprising manner. After that Saul automatically gave David an appointment over his army.

From that day Saul kept David with him and did not let him return to his father's house. Whatever Saul sent him to do, David did it so successfully that SAUL GAVE HIM A HIGH RANK IN THE ARMY. THIS PLEASED ALL THE PEOPLE, AND SAUL'S OFFICERS AS WELL.
                                                    1 Sam 18:2 NIV

When you ask for more responsibility and you perform every such task that may come your way diligently and excellently, your superiors or employers would develop trust in your capacity to deliver. The trust would grow to the point that if there is a job that needs to be done, you would immediately come to their minds as the guy who can do it. The more that happens, the more rewards would come your way. David became a high ranking officer in King Saul's army without necessarily rising through the ranks. He did not go for recruitment exercises but got admitted into the military because he asked for more responsibility and took the opportunity to deliver his best when it came. He got the best job in the King's military service without lobbying because he proved himself to be an asset by the currency of diligence.

Be ready for any opportunity that comes and be

ready to create opportunities when no one has shown up.

Every day brings with it fresh and new opportunities. No wonder William H. Burleigh said "there never was a day that did not bring its own opportunity for doing good that never could have been done before". Do not allow your chances and opportunities for greatness slip by without taking full advantage of them. A football coach whose team is losing an important football match by a one goal difference or is in a stalemate knows the importance of making the best use of opportunities. He is in a very good position to know the value of getting a penalty with just few minutes to stoppage time and converting that penalty. That is not a penalty any coach wants his player to miss knowing the fact that once that opportunity is missed, the chances of winning the cup that year would be lost. It would take an entire year of training and competing to ever come that close to winning the competition hence that opportunity is seen as golden. As golden as that opportunity may seem, many players fail to convert such an opportunity to victory. Only a player who has mastered the art of scoring a penalty under tension can convert such an opportunity. And it takes several hours, days, weeks, months and even years of diligent practice for a player to hone his scoring abilities in such a way that under last minute tension he would score a penalty. Hence every good coach prepares his players on how to convert penalties even when they are not likely to get a penalty in their next match. They know that when it matters most, the team should always be able to produce someone who can convert the penalties or else, they would only have themselves to blame. One of the reasons why some people tend to be ahead in life is that they make more out of the odds and ends of opportunities which many carelessly throw away. They make more out of seeming small opportunities that come their way compared to what others will get out of a whole life-time full of big opportunities.

Always hone your craft, sharpen your sword, dust your instruments and be ready for whatever opportunity may present itself on a daily basis. ***Do not wait for money before you start working on your ideas.*** That is the attitude of those who possess the currency of diligence. What we most times call a turning-point is simply an occasion which sums up and brings results out of previous training. When sudden advancements occur in a man's life, it seems strange to those who look from afar without proper observation. Such people begin to say things like "he was lucky to have got the promotion", "she was favoured to get the contract". While favour has its place in such big breaks, no one can take advantage of the opportunities which favour brings without adequate preparation. There are telltale signs which diligent preparation gives to observant watchers. When such signs and signals are traced, it becomes easy to understand the mystery behind some seeming sudden promotions. The life of Jesus was sometimes mysterious to His disciples and some onlookers because they would always see Him perform miracles when the opportunity presented itself. It took His disciples some time to notice that the miracles they saw in broad daylight were a product of Jesus' preparations sometimes at night and at other times, in His close fellowship with the Father. Sudden miracles only happen to men who expect and prepare for them or who have been trained to take advantage of the opportunities that bring them about. You want to earn in hundreds of millions and get big contracts with your business but you have no business name registered. You need to be intentional about it by registering your business in preparation for such an opportunity to come your way. It may not make sense at first that you are registering a business without any connections or business contacts. But as long as you have a vision to do business in a given area, you can begin to prepare yourself in any way possible.

Don't wait for the opportunity to come right at you before you start doing something definite that would push you closer to fulfilling your destiny. Create an opportunity for yourself especially if you discover that the opportunity you are waiting for is not forthcoming. George Stephenson was creating his opportunity when he mastered the rules of mathematics with a piece of chalk on the surface of the coal wagons in the mines where he worked. At 18, George realized the value of education and paid to study at a night school in order to learn reading, writing and arithmetic and that put an end to his illiteracy. Till date, he is acclaimed as the father of Railways. Those who lived in the days of Queen Victoria considered him to be a great example of diligence and thirst for improvement. He pioneered the invention of rail transport. His rail gauge is still a conventional measure and a standard for most of the world's rail. He created opportunities for himself by diligence despite the odds. You too can create opportunities for yourself by the currency of diligence.

Do not be weary in well doing.

One of the most honored inventors of all time was once a newsboy. He was responsible for the industrial regeneration of America but started out in life as an errand boy on the Grand Trunk Railway. There he sold food, sweets and newspaper to passengers. Thomas Alva Edison was then about fifteen years of age. He had already begun to invest himself in chemistry, and had fitted up a small itinerant laboratory which he made for himself at the back of the train. One day, as he was performing an experiment inside the moving train, and the train rounded a curve, the bottle of sulphuric acid broke. What followed was a fire as his laboratory went up in flames and there followed a series of complications. The conductor of the train promptly ejected the dedicated youth from the train. All of these defeating experiences never deterred Edison from his obsession with experiments. He went on to establish the world's first invention factory. This was located in Menlo Park, New Jersey. From there he began to develop several inventions that beggared the imagination of the men of his days. His inventions there gave him global fame and renown. You may be a student who studies hard for examinations but yet either fails, gets victimized or gets marginalized. That must not stop you. The schoolmaster at Edison's school thought he was too stupid and incredibly stubborn to learn anything meaningful. His mother however, seemed to have a different opinion on the matter. She was disgusted by the school and therefore took her son out. She then took it upon herself to school the young boy at home. There, she exposed him to books at a far higher level than anyone of his age. Under his mother's tutorship, Edison's horizons of knowledge were expanded beyond science into other fields of learning such as Philosophy, English, and History. By the time Thomas Edison was of age eleven, he established his own laboratory in the basement of his house[9]. Genius was built into Edison by his mother's diligent effort to school her boy right from home even when the school institution had given up on him.

Come to think of it, what would have become of Edison if he had no mother to stand up for him and put him through the learning curves of childhood? If you are a parent and your child seems not to be performing excellently at school, it means you have much work to do. Most of the great geniuses of all times like Albert Einstein, Thomas Edison and even Ben Carson emerged by reason of diligent parenting on the part of their respective mothers. As a parent you must not leave your child's mental development to the school teachers alone. You must be actively involved if you want to raise excellence out of your child. **The geniuses we hear of were made and sponsored by the currency of diligence.** Most times this currency had to be expended solely by the mothers, fathers or both parents without any support from the school systems.

Let us not become weary in doing good, for at the proper time WE WILL REAP A HARVEST IF WE DO NOT GIVE UP.

Gal 6:9 NIV

Thomas Edison made a very profound statement one time. He said, "Many of life's failures are people who did not realize how close they were to success when they gave up". Edison was an assiduous inventor who through diligence was able to keep working on his inventions until he got the right results and the best possible model for his time. He once said, "I have not failed. I've just found 1,000 ways that won't work". If he had given up at the five hundredth try and said it was impossible to invent the light bulb, the whole world would have believed it was a dead end and may even have acknowledged him for trying for five hundred times. But that was not the case. This inventor kept at his invention experiments diligently until he got the results he wanted. This man definitely understood the value of diligent work. Edison understood that a single invention was unlikely to make and sustain the sort of success he wanted, so he continued working, challenging, and pursuing new ideas well past the stage when many would have given up.

CHARGE
God has coded into your divine nature, the capacity for diligence. The truth is that everyone who is born again has the innate potential to exercise the qualities of diligence. The currency of diligence can be used as a currency of exchange for wealth, prosperity and global impact if it is invested properly and adequately in the right endeavour. This currency known as diligence produces results most when it is invested in your area of passion and strength. Be diligent in your business, profession, academics or whatever it is you are called to do or are gifted to accomplish and your story would become a life lesson to the generations that would witness your impact. Benjamin Franklin tried trading with the currency of diligence and in his lifetime he met with five kings and dined with one because of how great he became as a result. You too can engage the currency of diligence and your own story may be such that kings would seek you beyond what anyone has ever witnessed or imagined.

AFFIRMATIONS
I am diligent because I have the ability of God at work in me. I can do all things through Christ which strengthens me as long as it is within my areas of passion, calling and competence. I refuse to be lazy and to mortgage my destiny on the platform of procrastination. I work when it is time to work and I leisure when it is time for that. I do not squander my work hours on idle chatter and frivolous activities. My business is productive because of the investment of the currency of diligence which I make on it daily. I have the best jobs and contracts because I am reputed for thoroughness in everything I do. When I put in the slightest effort into my academics, business and

profession, I get optimum productivity. I do not overlabour myself and get little outcome in return. Whenever I work, I get great returns on my input. God is working mightily in me to convert my talent into a mega business via the currency of diligence. Blessed be the name of the Lord!

FOOD FOR THOUGHTS

There is a place for desire and passion if the currency of diligence needs to be invested in something.

- Do not wait for money before you start working on your ideas.

- The geniuses we hear of were made and sponsored by the currency of diligence.

- If you must seek help from others, ensure that you are not asking for bread but for seed.

- The difference between a lazy man and a diligent man is in the way they think.

- A lazy man invests his time, resources, energy and creativity digging out excuses and reasons why he cannot perform a task critical to his success and
- prosperity.

A diligent man channels all of his time, energy, resources and creativity towards finding a way around potential obstacles.

- Discovering purpose is not all that there is to achieving fulfillment but being tenacious in your pursuit of purpose is the key to accomplishment.

-

CHAPTER FOUR
THE CURRENCY OF
CHARACTER

"There is something infinitely better than to be a millionaire of money, and that is to be a millionaire of brains, of culture, of helpfulness to one's fellows, a millionaire of character."

Orison Swett Marden – Founder of Success Magazine.

What is Character?

According to Merriam Webster's dictionary, character is known as one of the attributes or features that make up and distinguish one individual from another. Character can be referred to as that which makes an individual or person stand out uniquely among other things. The word "characteristic" was derived from the word character, and that gives us an idea of the context in which this term character is being considered in this book. Every man possesses a unique personality which is a sum of his character. A man's character is formed by his beliefs, experiences and habits. Everybody has a character and each man's character contributes in forming that man's identity and image. Some people have a terrible character, while some have an admirable character. Either way, everyone attracts and repels people with his or her character both as an individual and as a business brand. It is unfortunate how a lot of people take for granted, the place of a good character personality in becoming a person of excellence. Character is critical to branding because character defines you before others.

Branding and Character

People do not buy products; they buy brands consciously or subconsciously, especially when they want to get good value for their money. A brand sends the message that expresses the characteristics of the product, service or individual who projects the image of the brand. A brand conveys to people the benefits they stand to receive from employing you, doing business with you or patronizing your goods and services. It tells potential customers what they can expect from your company, its products and services. It also tells them what they would get from you personally as an individual representing a brand. The truth is, everyone is either a brand or is representing one. ***Your brand is part of your identity and is another dimension to your character. Your brand is what differentiates you as a person from other individual brands.*** It differentiates the product and services you are offering from that of your competitors. Your brand is derived from who you are, who you want to be and who people perceive you to be. This speaks a lot about your identity, your self-concept and your character. All of these feature work together to form your product brand, service brand or personal brand.

People who get the best contracts and jobs are known for something that is hard to find anywhere. You must be very sensitive to what appeals to your target customers and what would trigger their buying decisions. When this is in place then you can brand your business in that direction.

David went out whithersoever Saul sent him, AND BEHAVED HIMSELF WISELY: and Saul set him over the men of war, and he was accepted in the sight of all the people, and also in the sight of Saul's servants.
1 Sam 18:5

Branding also involves masterfully positioning yourself in your niche market. It helps you to clearly define your target audience and know the best strategy that would reach out to them or attract them to you or your product and services. Your brand strategy is how, what, where, when and to whom you plan to communicate and deliver your brand messages. Where you advertise and the distribution channels you choose to employ is part of your brand strategy. The message you intend to send across, both visually and verbally, is also part of your brand strategy. Your brand identity gives you uniqueness and a competitive edge in the business market place. It is a summary of the added value of your company's products or services. This allows you to charge more for your brand than what identical, unbranded products command. That is why I said earlier that people buy brands and not products especially when quality is the buyer's priority. People would rather pay extra for a product or service from an excellent brand than to settle for a product with a poor brand or with no brand at all. The most obvious example of this is shopping for a product in a retail store like Shoprite and shopping for the same product in a roadside kiosk. People pay much more for what they buy in a supermarket like Shoprite than they would pay for that same product in a roadside kiosk. Why? Because Shoprite has built a powerful brand image and identity, it can charge more for its products and services and its target customers will gladly pay the higher price without a second thought.

The added value that goes with a brand gives it credibility. And when potential customers spot brand credibility, they immediately perceive the brand product to be of high quality and develop emotional attachment for that brand. This explains why some companies, for example, try to associate their products with celebrities, star athletes or a renowned public figure depending on their target audience. They spend so much to achieve that with the expectations that their potential customers and clients would transfer their emotional attachment from the public figure to their product. Most of the times, their expectations are not cut short. Defining your brand is like a journey on its own. Just the way every person needs to define himself, your business also needs a thorough definition of its unique identity. It may be a tasking endeavour but with serious thought and proper guidance, it is easy to outline. You need to answer some critical questions below to be able to develop a proper definition of your business brand: What is the vision for your business model? What are the needs your business intends to meet? What benefits would products or services provide? What do your clients and prospective customers already think of your business? What qualities do you want them to associate with your business? These require thorough and careful research on the needs, habits and desires of your clients and prospective customers. And don't rely on what you think they think. Know what they think. You also need to have a brand message. Your brand message should include the key messages you desire to pass across to your potential customers about your brand. Your brand message can also be used to communicate the core values of your business and personality. Integrate your brand and work it into every minute detail and aspect of your company.

Branding and Packaging

Branding even extends to every aspect of your business from how your phone lines are answered to what you or your salespeople wear on sales calls. Everything is supposed to be packaged intentionally, to convey the message of your brand. This is because small improvements in the packaging or external appearance of your product or service can often make a great deal of impact on your customers. Everything that the customer sees with his or her eyes from the first moment of contact with you, staffs or company, can affect the whole purchasing process. It can either attract them to make repeat purchases and to bring their friends or it can put them off totally. People form their first impression about you within the first few seconds of seeing you or seeing some element of your company.

Your packaging refers to the way your product or service appears from the outside. Packaging also refers to the way you and your people dress and groom. It refers to your offices, your waiting rooms, your brochures, your correspondence and every single visual element about your company. Bear in mind that everything counts when it comes to branding. Everything either helps or hurts. Everything boosts or lowers customer confidence in dealing with you. To build a successful and well packaged brand of a product or service, you must develop the habit of examining every visible aspect of the packaging of your product. Look through the eyes of your most critical customer and try to see your product or service from their perspectives. When referring to customers, there are different categories of customers. For someone who works in an office, your boss is your number one customer because you are working to satisfy his demands. While for the person running a business enterprise, your customers are those for whom your goods and services are delivered. In either case, character is crucial to creating a lasting impression on your customers. Goods and services have features or characteristics they possess, and these characteristics provide the customers some special benefits that could either make them keep coming back to you or keep them away. Sam Walton, the man who founded Walmart, once said, "We all have one boss, the customer. And she can fire us any time she wants by simply deciding to shop somewhere else." This makes it important to always make the right impression on customers whenever the opportunity arises.

Achieving Excellence by the Currency of Character

> Decide what legacy you want to be remembered for and begin to act accordingly now.

There is a very fascinating story about a man named Alfred Nobel. He was a Swedish chemist, engineer, inventor, businessman, and philanthropist. He was known for inventing the dynamite. Nobel also owned a company called Bofors, which had become a major manufacturer of cannon and other armaments. This man was a great inventor with 355 different patents to his name and the dynamite was the most famous of them all. Many years ago, Ludvig Nobel, the brother of Alfred Nobel died in Stockholm. But somehow, the newspapers got the name wrong and published articles saying that it was Alfred Nobel himself who had died in error. They then wrote his obituary, which Alfred Nobel read in the papers the next day. As he read the obituary the next day, He noticed that the major achievement for which he was remembered was for the invention of gunpowder. Despite his other inventions, he was only remembered for the invention which had been responsible for the death of numerous people in wars, uprisings and conflicts all around the world. One French newspaper in the same misinformation published an article about his premature obituary which they titled "Le marchand de la mort est mort" which translates as "The merchant of death is dead". When Alfred Nobel read the obituary, he was horrified at the idea that he would be remembered in this way. This obituary made such a great impact on Alfred Nobel that he immediately began to rearrange his life just so that he could change his legacy. After reading the premature obituary which condemned him for deriving profit from the sales of arms, he handed down his entire fortune using it to institute the famous Nobel Prizes award. At this writing, Nobel Prize has awarded 584 prizes to about 923 laureates, and they receive huge prize money and a gold medal both worth millions of dollars[1]. He became very careful to ensure that when he truly dies, his real obituary, would be written in a completely different light. In order to achieve this, he established the Nobel Prizes, based on his great fortune, which are today the highest awards that can be attained in the worlds of literature, medicine, science, economics, peace and chemistry. By thinking clearly about the legacy he wanted to leave, he transformed both his present actions, and his ultimate memory. He rewrote his own obituary. Today, the synthetic element called nobelium was named after him.

Think about the legacies you want to leave behind as a person. Also think about the good legacies you want your business to be remembered for when you are no more. The moment you can do that, start today and begin to arrange your life in that order and direction. Live your life today with a conscious focus on the legacies you want the next generation to build upon and take after you. Act accordingly now in a way that would produce the memory that you desire people to have of you in the future. Tomorrow belongs to those who can take a hold of today. This would go a long way to affect the way you would lead your life. Alfred Noble took a hold of his tomorrow by his decision to posthumously donate the majority of his wealth to found the Nobel Prize. This great act of his has touched so many lives and families all around the world. And it came about because he wanted to leave behind a better legacy.

◦ **Develop a stable character**

Benjamin Franklin was a man who by virtue of his exceptional character, and excellent personality, distinguished himself in the history of the United States of America. He became the first millionaire in the United States of America. As a young man, Benjamin Franklin felt that he was not well cultured enough to project the kind of image he would have wanted for himself. He thought he was ill mannered, had a rough behavior and was kind of argumentative. He began to notice that his poor attitudes and behaviors were causing his colleagues, coworkers and business associates to become hostile toward him. He therefore made up his mind to rewrite the script of his own personality in such a way that he could cause a change in his character. He made a list of 13 virtues that he felt the ideal person should possess. He then focused on developing in himself one of these virtues each week. He did this all week long, as he went about his daily affairs, he kept reminding himself to practice the particular virtue he was working on. Whether it was temperance, tolerance or tranquility, he kept cultivating these attributes into his character personality. Over time, as Benjamin Franklin developed these virtues, they became a part of his character. Before long, he became one of the most popular personalities and statesmen of his time. He became such a respected and influential personality, in Paris as an Ambassador from the United States during the Revolutionary War. He was also one of the major figures of influence during the Constitutional Convention, when the United States Constitution and the Bill of Rights were debated, negotiated and agreed upon[2]. By working on himself to cultivate the habits of an excellent person, he made himself into a person who ended up charting the course of the history of America. He is still respected till today as one of the founding fathers of the United States of America because of his exceptional character and personality.

Gain control over your emotions

The starting point of achieving excellence in character is to have a strong grip on your emotions. Gaining mastery of one's emotions through self control is critical to developing excellence. Many great and influential leaders who have gained global recognition have been disgraced by their emotions because they lost control of themselves. There was once a president of the United States of America who tainted his impeccable image by condescending to having sexual affairs with a white house intern. Even though this man had a knack for leadership and displayed exceptional leadership skill as a president, he lost his respect the moment the news of his secret affair went out in the airwaves. If you cannot control your emotions and cravings, you would be prone to different kinds of assaults, both on your credibility and personality. That is what Solomon explained in the scripture below.

A person without self-control is like a city with broken-down walls.
Prov 25:28

One of the most important goals every kingdom citizen needs to deliberately strive to accomplish in the course of life on earth is to become an excellent person. Not just excellent in skill but also in character and in the mastery of emotions. Scripture is replete with several examples of people who did not handle their emotions properly. David is one of such examples; Esau is yet another example, and a host of others.

The moment they allowed their emotions control their actions, they lost a lot of valuables that even money could not buy. Worthy of note is the story of Reuben, a man who was described as having great potentials to excel. Due to his instability of character, he placed a barricade on his own prospects.

Reuben, you are my firstborn, my might, the first sign of my strength, excelling in honor, excelling in power. TURBULENT AS THE WATERS, YOU WILL NO LONGER EXCEL, for you went up onto your father's bed, onto my couch and defiled it.

Gen 49:3-4 NIV

Reuben had an unstable character and that cost him a whole lot. The Bible likened him to water because of some attributes of water. Water has very unstable molecules which are always undergoing molecular vibrations and movements. Reuben lacked stability of character and that was why he was described as being unstable and turbulent as water. Mark the words that followed the description of his unstable and turbulent character. The words say that he will no longer excel despite the fact that he was the firstborn with all the benefits and rights that were his by reason of being the first child. Despite the fact that he was strong, powerful and thus commanded honour among his brethren, he lost his place in destiny because of his weak character. He could not control his emotions and by reason of that defiled his father's bed.

Getting the Best Jobs and Contracts by the Currency of

Character

Have a good report

Your character can either make or mar you in the run for a successful career. Your character is something that can be used to distinguish you for the best spot in life. It matters how you act to people and how you treat them. This can go a long way to create lasting impressions on people that would be so difficult to forget. Your character can bring to you opportunities that you never bargained for. No wonder Paul states that anyone who desires the office of a bishop must be a person of good report. When you have a good character, you would always have a good report because you have made a good impression on those you encounter. The office of a bishop that Paul spoke about in scripture is an administrative office. In giving Timothy the criteria and qualities to look out for in selection, Paul tells Timothy to ensure that whoever is chosen is someone of good report. That means the kind of report that people have of you based on the character you displayed to them would go a long way to open doors you cannot even imagine.

This is a true saying, IF A MAN DESIRE THE OFFICE OF A BISHOP, HE DESIRETH A GOOD WORK. MOREOVER HE MUST HAVE A GOOD REPORT of them which are without;

1 Tim 3:1, 7 KJV

It is not enough to desire a fantastic contract, business deal, or a promotion at your place of work; you need to have a good report to get there. And this good report is not the kind that comes in by sharp practices. It is that kind of report that comes from a genuine track record of consistency in performance and character. There are people who have landed themselves great opportunities because they displayed enviable traits that projected them in the best light before people who had the capacity to help them to the next levels of their careers and businesses. In the early church, there came a need for recruitment of some people to take on new jobs in order to meet the expansion needs of the church at that time. This led the twelve disciples to ask for the people to select appointees; and again one of the fundamental criteria for selection is that they be people who are of good report.

And in those days, when the number of the disciples was multiplied, there arose a murmuring of the Grecians against the Hebrews, because their widows were neglected in the daily ministration. Then the twelve called the multitude of the disciples unto them, and said, It is not reason that we should leave the word of God, and serve tables. WHEREFORE, BRETHREN, LOOK YE OUT AMONG YOU SEVEN MEN OF HONEST REPORT, full of the Holy Ghost and wisdom, WHOM WE MAY APPOINT OVER THIS BUSINESS. And the saying pleased the whole multitude: AND THEY CHOSE STEPHEN, a man full of faith and of the Holy Ghost, and Philip, and Prochorus, and Nicanor, and Timon, and Parmenas, and Nicolas a proselyte of Antioch:

Acts 6:1-4, 5 KJV

The term good report according to its Greek rendering also refers to one who has a good testimony in the mouth of others or one who is well reported of by people around. The people of the early church chose seven men to occupy the vacancies without these men putting forward any initial interest. Nobody wants to entrust his business or enterprise to someone who has a bad reputation around an industry or in the society. Everyone wants to do business with people of character, men of integrity and credibility. This is why most people take a look at testimonials of products and services before making buying decisions. In the same way, people also give an ear to the kind of genuine reports that people give concerning you. You may not know but people are watching you both consciously and unconsciously. That is why it matters the way you treat people anywhere you find yourself. You never know the opportunities you have closed due to a negative attitude or behavior you sometimes display. ***May you not fall into the trap of ruining your career or business prospects due to a character currency deficiency syndrome in Jesus name!***

George Washington, was the first President of the United States. He was also the General in Command of the American army, and he led them to victory in the Revolutionary war against the British army. He was greatly admired and adored for the quality of his character, the graciousness of his manners, and correctness of behavior. Interestingly, George Washington did not start off in life possessing all of these excellent qualities. He was a young man who was raised in a middle class family, with few advantages. His life was going to take a new turn when he came across a little book entitled "The Rules of Civility and Decent Behavior in Company and Conversation." As a teenage boy, he copied these 110 rules into a personal notebook because he had aspirations to succeed and prosper. He carried that notebook with him every day and constantly reviewed them throughout his life. By practicing the "Rules of Civility," he developed in himself an excellent character, accompanied with a very admirable behavior[3]. His manners played a huge role in causing him to win the hearts of his countrymen. He deliberately molded, practiced and repeated the habits that he most desired to make a part of his character. Eventually, George Washington became in every respect a man of excellence and of good report. He made a conscious effort to cultivate the character and behavioral pattern he needed to develop in order to become the kind of man he wanted to become. Imagine that you are being watched with hidden cameras and at the end of the month or the year a reward would be given to the person with the best attitude towards work. How would you take your job? How would you behave if you knew that you were being watched and that your next level of promotion depended on your behavior when it looked like no one else was watching? Whether the hidden camera idea is true or not, someone somewhere is watching you and considering you for a big time opportunity even when you least expect it. Always be conscious of this so that you can leave a good and lasting impression on people who may later be of help to you, your business and career.

Building a Global Business Brand with the Currency of Character

Discover your Unique Selling Proposition (USP)

This is a very important aspect of business that must be thoroughly looked at if you really want your business to blossom. The unique selling proposition is that one trait or skill which your business brand, product or service possesses that differentiates it from others. The USP states your unique value or competitive advantage and makes it known to either your customers or to people in your organization. It is a value that is unique to your brand that no other individual or company can offer.

Many new entrepreneurs and business owners do not know how to determine their unique selling point. In the midst of thousands and even hundreds of thousands of businesses or brands in your industry, not having a unique selling point or not knowing what it is about is too costly. This could lead to a business getting lost in the crowd and the eventual death of the business. This is so because, without USP no business would be able to attract the pool of customers required to grow that business and to keep it afloat. One thing that the USP does is that it states the benefits that potential customers would gain from either patronizing or associating with a particular business. It helps the customer answer the question, "What do I stand to gain from this brand that I cannot get elsewhere?" Your selling point as a brand or a business must be driven towards a particular need which your business has come to provide quicker, easier and better answers to. Jesus Christ is a unique example as far as the unique selling proposition is concerned. When He stated His unique selling point one time in a synagogue full of potential patrons of His personal brand, the Bible records that everyone fastened their eyes on Him. They were looking intently to find out what benefits He had to offer and what was in Him for them. He left them without doubts as He stated His selling point articulately.

When he came to the village of Nazareth, his boyhood home, he went as usual to the synagogue on the Sabbath and stood up to read the Scriptures. The scroll of Isaiah the prophet was handed to him. He unrolled the scroll and found the place where this was written: "THE SPIRIT OF THE LORD IS UPON ME, FOR HE HAS ANOINTED ME TO BRING GOOD NEWS TO THE POOR. HE HAS SENT ME TO PROCLAIM THAT CAPTIVES WILL BE RELEASED, THAT THE BLIND WILL SEE, THAT THE OPPRESSED WILL BE SET FREE, AND THAT THE TIME OF THE LORD'S FAVOR HAS COME." He rolled up the scroll, handed it back to the attendant, and sat down. ALL EYES IN THE SYNAGOGUE LOOKED AT HIM INTENTLY.

Luke 4:16-21

Notice how Jesus stated in clear terms the benefits He had to offer and to whom He offered these benefits. Also observe the way He held them spell bound as He stated His selling points. The people in the synagogue were apparently interested and captivated by Jesus because His benefits were customer centered. They were targeted toward meeting specific needs. **Your unique selling proposition must be customer centered for it to attract customers to your business or brand.** Most people do not take this into account when branding or selling their product. They assume their customers would like a product because they like it and hence their businesses do not attract the desired customers and clients. Jesus always took every opportunity to differentiate Himself from the numerous religious leaders of His days. He made it clear what His uniqueness was and for Jesus, there was never a basis for competition because He was in a class of His own. This was why a lot of people were drawn toward his brand despite being affiliated with other inferior brands in the form of a religious leader or priest. Today, there are about 2.4 billion followers of Jesus Christ and still counting because, nobody else on earth living or dead, can ever and would ever be able to offer salvation to humanity. But Jesus has given salvation as part of the many other benefits of His brand. You too must be able to set yourself or your business brand apart if you intend to stand out and build a global business brand. To achieve that, you need to discover your unique selling point.

Take advantage of feedbacks

If you are going to build a global business brand, it means you need to be ready to deal with many different customer challenges. Inasmuch as you would begin to see results and receive some profit depending on the nature of the business, you would also encounter some challenges. You would be dealing with personalities that cut across gender, race, culture, climate, colour and educational status. These are people with different mindsets and perspectives to life in general. For your business to be a global brand, it has to have all of these people including their peculiarities in view. You can use to advantage, the feedbacks you would get in the process of trying to deliver your business benefits across to these people. Your business growth is tied to the ability to integrate feedbacks into your business. This helps your business improve to the point where it can meet potential customers at their level without compromising standards. The moment you start providing business services to people, one thing you should look out for is feedback. This feedback could be in the form of a testimonial, an advice, a suggestion, and even a criticism. We love it when we get positive feedbacks like money, testimonies, an award, a reward or a promotion. But when we get other kinds of feedback which I believe is more important for improvement to take place, we react to them with the wrong attitude. When we get criticized, graded poorly or ranked lowly, we do not like it and this is a normal feeling. But if you want your business to grow and improve, reaching and touching more lives, you must learn to respond with the right attitude to criticisms even though it does not feel nice. See them as pointers to ways by which you can improve yourself or product and move on.

Running into a deficit and not being able to make profit is a negative feedback that does not feel good when talked about especially if you love to see the growth of your business. But beyond the feeling, it is also an indication that something is not right. It gives you a red alert signal that you are headed in the wrong direction. When you get a "check" sign on the dashboard of your Mercedes jeep, what do you do? Would you get mad at the sensors for the somewhat negative sign? On the contrary, you would begin to wonder what could have gone wrong to warrant such a signal and then you would probably take the car to an auto mechanic to help rectify the problem. If you should ignore the signal, your vehicle may breakdown on the way and that is what happens when you ignore negative results and check signs in your business. When you notice that your Range Rover Sports is not as efficient as you think it should be, what do you do? If you are a responsible owner of that vehicle, you would do all you can to check it out and make it more efficient with an improved performance. That is the same way we should respond to low rankings, poor grades, criticisms, and negative insights from our customers and colleagues. We can use them to our advantage by not ignoring them and not allowing them get to us in any way that is not productive. Whether we seek for it or not, we always get reports from people in different forms. If you learn to listen to these reports and feedbacks from our clients, customers, family, friends or even your bank manager, you would get signals on what aspects of your business needs improvement.

You also need to be careful with feedback, both positive and negative ones, because not all feedbacks are worth giving attention. Some are actually biased and insincere with their feedbacks, whether it is a praise, commendation or criticism. Try to run a background check on the credibility of the source or the transparency of the report before giving it any serious attention. Also watch out for patterns and repetitive trends in feedbacks, reports, criticisms and commendations. As the Bible even tells us that in the mouth of two or three witnesses, every word is established. If you are getting the same pattern of feedbacks from more than three sources under different circumstances, then that feedback must be treated with urgent attention. Always try to learn from feedbacks and insights whether positive or negative. Thank those who give you sincere feedbacks with a heart that sees improvement opportunities in every positive or negative report.

Keys for Converting the Currency of Character into Tangible Wealth

Build a good name.

Every business has a name synonymous to it by reason of the value it offers to people. As long as that name remains a household name which is not only known by a great amount of people, but is also known for something good, people would want to be associated with the name. Money is not everything because there are some things that money must answer to and one of those things is a good name. It takes a lot to build a name for yourself both in business, career or in life generally. The fortunes of some businesses have been lost because they compromised their standards in exchange for making some more money than usual. Some persons have lost their careers because of the stigma of a bad name they carry around. Imagine a top staff of a reputable company being nabbed for fraudulent practices or for theft with his name published for other companies to be on the alert. No matter how skilled or talented that individual is, he may never get another job in any other establishment within his industry. Never engage in practices that would mortgage your name for immediate gratification. It takes the currency of character to maintain discipline in the face of stiff temptations that demands you to compromise your values. For example, a customer comes into a retail store where you work as a sales representative and somehow overpays for his groceries without knowing. It takes a sales representative who has character and is disciplined to refund the extra cash to the customer. That gesture alone can make that customer become a client. **Customers come and go, but when a customer becomes a client, he stays with your business, brings his friends along and grows with you.** A client would go out of his way to bring more customers to you through word of mouth by reason of a kind gesture done to him. They would respect your character and keep coming back to patronize your goods and services for what it is worth. To attain this requires discipline and a solid character.

A GOOD NAME IS RATHER TO BE CHOSEN THAN GREAT RICHES, and loving favour rather than silver and gold.

Prov 22:1-2

I have even heard of stories where a sales representative at a retail store got a wonderful job, ten times better than his previous one because he refunded extra cash to an unsuspecting customer. The job was granted him without having to apply or perform any other formality. His character was his leverage. Your character is an important virtue that can affect the customer's perception of you, your goods and services. It contributes to what makes for a good or a bad reputation or name. There is no better advertisement than a good reputation. Most of the world's greatest companies, brands and manufacturers esteem their reputation to be their most treasured possession. Vast sums of money are paid for the use of a name in a franchise agreement because of its reputation for integrity and excellence. Having a good name or reputation can bring a lot of financial gains especially when you have remained consistent over a good period of time. Do not take for granted the kind of reputation and report that you send out through your behavior at work or the attitude which you display about your business. It would go a long way to determine how well and how far you can go as a businessman or professional.

Save diligently for future expansion:

There is a popular saying that "it takes money to make money". This saying seems to suggest that it is not possible to become wealthy from the scratch with nothing down. But I have discovered that this idea produces a very wrong mentality which only the understanding of kingdom currency can correct. The truth is that it takes kingdom currency to make money in any earthly currency. You can go from nothing to something if you possess kingdom currency. But if you lack kingdom currency, even though you possess everything, it is only a matter of time before it tends to nothingness. This needs to be properly understood because when it is not, saving may become meaningless especially if you do not have a big cash flow.

When the currency of character is in place, you would not just save because you have extra money but you would save because it is a discipline that attracts more to you no matter how little it is that you can save per period. *It is not the money you can save as much as the character and discipline that is developed while saving that brings about financial prosperity.* Possessing wealth without financial discipline is likely going to end up as a disaster. If you cannot save money when you have it coming to you in trickles, you would never be able to save when it comes to you in abundance. It is like expecting a crawling child to start running when he is yet to master the art of walking. In the same vein, you have to walk before you run. It is only when you can get your finances under control at a low level that you can demonstrate your ability to manage and grow money at a higher level. It takes character, discipline and dedication to save money when you have lots of needs calling for your attention. It takes diligence to keep storing up a given amount of money when you wish you could spend it. There are many people who work extremely hard to make money and end up spending the money they have managed to make on frivolities.

The man William Clement Stone was known to be one of the mentors of Jack Canfield. Through the principles learned from William Stone, Jack Canfield went on to become America's number one success coach at this writing and bestselling co-author of the Chicken Soup for the Soul series. William Clement Stone himself started off as a penniless paperboy on the streets of Chicago, and went on to amass a fortune of $800 Million (USD) in his lifetime. This man once said, "If you cannot save money, then the seeds of greatness are not in you." Why is it that saving money is so important? It is because saving money is a discipline, and it requires persistence of purpose and consistency of action to produce results. The thing about the discipline of saving money is that it affects all other disciplines in your life. For example, the moment you decide to save money, it means you are telling yourself that you would resist every other temptation to spend the money. That requires character, discipline and a great level of persistence.

Go to the ant, you sluggard; consider its ways and be wise! It has no commander, no overseer or ruler, yet it stores its provisions in summer and gathers its food at harvest.

Prov 6:6-8 NIV

I must confess that saving is not an easy task especially when it is something you are not used to. It is something that takes a lot of personal discipline to accomplish because it requires consistency and resilience. That is why Solomon, the wisest king of old tells us to learn from the ants. They have no commander but yet save toward their future year in year out. The ants have been able to develop in themselves character such that even in the absence of a commander, they seem to know how important saving is to their survival. **If you do not have the discipline to refrain from spending all the money you earn, then you are simply not qualified to become wealthy.** If you are not constant and consistent towards saving, you may not achieve much with the monies that come into your hands every now and then. If by some streak of luck or by chance you do become wealthy, but lack the character, discipline and self-control, that money would disappear because you would not be capable of holding onto it. This is why most lottery winners often go bankrupt and are back at their old jobs within two to three years of winning big amounts of monies. This also explains why most overnight successes are broke and back living in one bedroom apartments. This happens because they did not develop the character for prosperity through the discipline of saving.

CHARGE
Never take for granted the place of character in building a

personal brand or a business brand. Allow people know you for good things only, by being stable and consistent in character. It is very important how you brand yourself as a professional or businessman. This is because it affects people's perception about you and what they can get from associating with you or your business. People are watching out for you in ways you do not know. There are hidden cameras everywhere watching you secretly without your knowledge. Be a person of good report because you never know what opportunities may come your way. You are just one good report away from a mega job or a major contract which you did not even seek for.

AFFIRMATIONS
I have the character of Christ and it is coded into everything I do. It is reflected in the kind of business I do and in how I do business. I am a person of character and I have the attitude of a winner. I am a lifelong learner hence I take advantage of every opportunity to improve on my character and brand myself for excellence. The currency of character is heavily at work in my profession and my place of work for good. I am branded after the image and likeness of Christ for the best jobs in my industry. I build a global business brand with the ideas and innovations brought unto me by the Spirit of God. I am not a failure and I refuse to be confused. I am known for good things at school, my place of work and in business because I am branded for exploits by the grace of God. Glorious things are spoken of me everywhere I go and in everything I do. Thank you Lord because you have endowed me with the

currency of character and I trade with it productively in Jesus name!

FOOD FOR THOUGHTS

- Your brand is part of your identity and is another dimension to your character. Your brand is what differentiates you as person from other individual brands.

- Your unique selling proposition must be customer centered for it to attract customers to your business or brand.

- Customers come and go, but when a customer becomes a client, he stays with your business, brings his friends along and grows with you.

- If you do not have the discipline to refrain from spending all the money that you earn, then you are simply not qualified to become wealthy.

- It is not the money you can save as much as the character and discipline that is developed while saving that brings about financial prosperity.

CHAPTER FIVE
THE CURRENCY OF
A GOOD NETWORK

"Networking is an essential part of building wealth".

Armstrong Williams

There is a famous saying that "no man is an island." How true that is! People who work alone are extremely limited in the growth and level of success they attain. People who work in isolation can never reach the highest possible levels of accomplishment. People who do not work with people but work against people's successes would also never succeed. God designed the world in such a manner that many things work in an interconnected and interdependent fashion. God arranged for man to always function in a networking environment in order to achieve greater results with less effort. No wonder the Bible tells us that one person can chase a thousand but when two people come together, they would put ten thousand to flight instead of two thousand. This is so, partly because each individual has a network of people who are within his influence. And when these two individuals harmonize their resources towards the same goal and in a productive manner there is so much that can be achieved. I believe more people would turn out successful at a faster pace if they committed themselves to building a formidable network in any field of life's endeavour.

What is a Network?
The word network has taken on different meanings especially with the recent advancement in the computer and technology age. But the context we shall be considering when referring to network in this chapter is with respect to a "people network". In the light of that, a network can be seen as a group of people who are interconnected in different ways and by reason of that are parts of a system. These people make their contribution to the accomplishment of the primary goals of the major players in the system.

In a society where businesses are getting revolutionized by the impact of social media on reaching out to people, the value of a good network has become clearer than ever before. Have you ever wondered why people would pay thousands of dollars to make their businesses go viral on social media? Have you ever wondered why brands such as individuals, businesses, establishments and even churches develop sponsored contents on social media in order to reach more people and to grow their network? It is not because they do not have other important things to do with money but rather because they know the implication of getting their content in the face of more people. They know the value of building people networks through information sharing.

Michele Janae described networking as "the act of exchanging information with people who can help you professionally". Networking is not about just connecting people. It's about connecting people with people, people with ideas, and people with opportunities. Most of the global business brands the world has ever seen have been built as a result of the network of people who worked seamlessly to bring their goals to fruition. The greater the network, the greater results and rewards that can be realized so long as the network is properly harnessed. The world today has become a global village and networking with people has become a lot easier than it was several decades ago. We are all part of one network or the other whether we know it or not. The quality of a network is tantamount to the quality of people in that network.

Getting the Best Jobs and Contracts by the Currency of a Good Network

- Proper positioning for business and career opportunities

There are many great people, who would never be known by anyone beyond their family members. This is because they only display their greatness inside their closets. The only people who know what they are capable of and who benefit from their gifts and talent are their family members. Such people are never going to experience global spread because of improper positioning. There are many athletes and footballers who would remain unknown because none of the people that matter in that system of people have ever seen their talent or heard of them. No matter who you are and where you are from, you need a good network of people who believe in your brand for your business to blossom. That is why it matters who you associate with. Everyone who wants to get the best jobs without application and, or build a global business brand must position himself properly in a most strategic manner. Some people never emerge in their area of calling, vision and passion because they have not been able to identify their key customers. They are yet to locate those who know their value and would appreciate their worth. **Building a good network is an investment in business**. It is also an asset that a person can leverage on for global brand spread.

It takes time however to grow a sustainable network, but when it is done properly, it can yield great results for years to come. There are people who pay big to fly first class to their destinations. Even though they know they could pay five to ten times less if they fly with economy class, they still choose to travel with first class. They do that because they know the quality of people they would connect with in the first class cabin. They know that they stand a good chance of connecting with people who stand a great chance of boosting their network and ultimately their businesses. They stand the chance of positioning themselves as a brand before high quality people who may likely be interested in their product or service and would be both capable and willing to pay for it. They end up meeting people who give them contracts or business engagements worth twenty times more than what they paid to fly first class. A lot of mega businesses and mega contacts have been established in the first class section of aircrafts. This is because when people meet you there, they assume that you too, are as important as they are. They even become curious about who you are and why you're as lavish as they are to pay such an inflated price for the flight. This is not to say you cannot meet the right people without flying first class. It is just an illustration of the fact that proper positioning is critical to having and making valuable contacts that could make a difference in your career and business. For example, if a jobless man keeps hanging out with fellow jobless men, the chances are, they would remain jobless till God knows when. They would sit together every day, lamenting and complaining about their situation to each other. But when a jobless man hangs out and makes contacts with people who are job givers and not job seekers, the chances are that by reason of positioning, they would not stay jobless for long.

▪ Stay visible when it matters most

There is a very amazing story of a rich man who had a disadvantaged height. He wanted to meet with the Chief Executive Officer of the whole universe known as Jesus Christ. Being a very short and stout man, he was disadvantaged. He knew that would hinder his chances of ever meeting with the Master of the universe. This man taught us a very critical lesson about positioning when he ran ahead and climbed a tree. By reason of the way he positioned himself, he was noticed by the Master despite the crowd and he got the chance to meet with him.

Jesus entered Jericho and was passing through. A man was there by the name of Zacchaeus; he was a chief tax collector and was wealthy. He wanted to see who Jesus was, but being a short man he could not, because of the crowd. SO HE RAN AHEAD AND CLIMBED A SYCAMORE-FIG TREE TO SEE HIM, since Jesus was coming that way. WHEN JESUS REACHED THE SPOT, HE LOOKED UP AND SAID TO HIM, "ZACCHAEUS, COME DOWN IMMEDIATELY. I MUST STAY AT YOUR HOUSE TODAY." So he came down at once and welcomed him gladly.

Luke 19:1-6 NIV

Zacchaeus knew that it would be a total waste of time to join the crowd because he had no height and no might to press through the crowd. Even if he did, he knew that he would not get the necessary attention which he needed to get from the Master. He therefore changed his playing field and remembered that if he could distinguish himself from the crowd by gaining visibility, he would "steal the show". He got Jesus' attention by staying visible. Visibility is the reason why companies pay heavily for advert placements and billboards yearly. They understand that if they can come out of the pool of businesses scrambling for the attention of customers, they would be able to distinguish themselves in a way that would catch the attention of their target customers. In the same vein you need to stay visible so that the right people who would benefit from your skills and from the value you have to offer gets to see you.

You are the light of the world. A city on a hill cannot be hidden. NEITHER DO PEOPLE LIGHT A LAMP AND PUT IT UNDER A BOWL. INSTEAD THEY PUT IT ON ITS STAND, AND IT GIVES LIGHT TO EVERYONE IN THE HOUSE. In the same way, let your light shine before men, that they may see your good deeds and praise your Father in heaven.

Matt 5:14-16 NIV

Even Jesus the King of the kingdom of heaven understood the value of positioning in building a strong and viable network which can be used as a medium of exchange for brand awareness and business profitability. In the above scripture, He told us that nobody lights a lamp and places it in a position where no one would benefit from it. He divulged some vital secrets in that verse by telling us that in order to reach the right kind of people who could be potential customers, or potential employers, we must understand the place of strategic positioning. If you desire to have maximum results for the value you add, and the benefits you offer, visibility and proper positioning is a critical factor to that. Whenever we light up our candles and we want it to give light to the whole room, we position it in the best spot for more reach. We do not hide it under the table where its value would not be benefitted from. In much the same way, we must display our value before people who would appreciate it and by so doing our people network would grow and expand more.

- **Maintain viable relationships with vision oriented and likeminded people**

The more people you know, and the more people who know you in a positive way and for a positive reason, the more chances there are that you would succeed at anything you do. God reaches men through men. He places people on your path to greatness and makes them instruments that would be of help to you either consciously or even without their knowing. Just one person you meet at the right place and right time can be the one that would open up opportunities that could transform your whole life. That is why you must not take some important relationships for granted. People are great assets and blessings in disguise if you know their value. You never know a man's worth until you really know who is in his network. And sometimes you may never know who he would become several years from now. Someone you took for granted when you had the power to help could become the governor of your state or the employer of your child tomorrow. If you did not treat that person appropriately when you had the chance. It may be to your detriment. In time to come when that person becomes better placed or more accomplished, you may not be able to benefit from his network. Then you may regret ever maltreating such a potential game changer in your network. The three Hebrew boys benefitted greatly from being a part of Daniel's network because they maintained a viable relationship with him. By reason of that, when Daniel got promoted, he recommended them to the king for other key positions which they did not even apply for or dream of getting. Because they had a good and viable working relationship with Daniel, it landed them that choice appointment.

Then King Nebuchadnezzar fell prostrate before Daniel and paid him honor and ordered that an offering and incense be presented to him. The king said to Daniel, "Surely your God is the God of gods and the Lord of kings and a revealer of mysteries, for you were able to reveal this mystery." THEN THE KING PLACED DANIEL IN A HIGH POSITION AND LAVISHED MANY GIFTS ON HIM. He made him ruler over the entire province of Babylon and placed him in charge of all its wise men. MOREOVER, AT DANIEL'S REQUEST THE KING APPOINTED SHADRACH, MESHACH AND ABEDNEGO ADMINISTRATORS OVER THE PROVINCE

OF BABYLON, WHILE DANIEL HIMSELF REMAINED AT THE ROYAL COURT.

Dan 2:46-49 NIV

This is not to say that you should start looking for people who are highly connected to befriend in order to get a job or contract. You may devalue yourself by doing that. Just be sensitive to people and be of help to them when you can, meet new people when the opportunity to do so comes. When you begin to add value to people at any level, you would attract people with like minds who would want to add value to you in return. They could do that by connecting you to the right channels and resources. Some people are wealthy without knowing. And some people are poor because they do not understand that God has given them wealth in disguise by virtue of the quality of people in their network. They may not have anything in the bank but they may have wonderful contacts in their network that may be willing to collaborate with them or recommend them for a promotion when the need arises. These contacts are not necessarily there to give you bread money to spend on luxuries and reckless squander. They may never give you money, but could bring opportunities for wealth generation your way, if the relationship is properly harnessed. These contacts can also remain there and stay underutilized or even unutilized if not properly harnessed. Begin to harness your people network productively and watch God catapult you unto greatness.

Building a Global Business Brand with the Currency of a Good Network

- **Expand your network**

The greatest way to expand your network is by meeting new

people from different walks of life. Understanding the way they think and their mentality gives you an idea of how people in their own network may be wired to think. Always try to look for ways by which you can tailor your product for new audiences and niches. The moment your product works for someone in the banking sector, you automatically have expanded your network to banks and its staffs. Probably you are a tailor or fashion designer, the moment you make a particular attire for a politician; you stand the chance of getting more politicians to ask for the same kind of design from you. So never take for granted opportunities to network with people across different walks of life. Always look for ways you can tailor your products and services to new markets and customer targets. Study their behaviours, likes and dislikes and pattern your product in a way that appeals to them. The moment you do this, you have expanded your business into a new network.

As soon as they got out of the boat, people recognized Jesus. They ran throughout that whole region and carried the sick on mats to wherever they heard he was. And wherever he went — into villages, towns or countryside — they placed the sick in the marketplaces. They begged him to let them touch even the edge of his cloak, and all who touched him were healed.

Mark 6:54-56 NIV

Jesus expanded the network of His ministry toward the sick in a unique way immediately after the woman with the issue of blood had touched the hem of his garment and received her healing (Mark 5:28-34). Immediately she received her healing by touching his garments, a vast network of sick people who preferred the idea of touching His garment to receive their healing came after Him. That woman introduced into Jesus' business (ministry), a new network of people with different preferences. Be very sensitive to opportunities that would open your business to new networks.

▪ Expand your business through referrals

One of the ways to grow your business especially if you offer a product or service that people buy once in a long period of time is through good referrals. For example, if you are an author, it means people can only buy a particular book authored by you over a given period of time. They would hardly come back to buy that particular book except they were to buy it for other people. In that case you need to have an expanded distribution network. You also need people who would appreciate your products enough to refer it to other people within their own network. That kind of referral comes when you offer high end products and services as an author or as a business person. Jesus expanded His Father's business by the use of the referral method. The story below shows us how He did it:

Just then his disciples returned and were surprised to find him talking with a woman. But no one asked, "What do you want?" or "Why are you talking with her?" Then, leaving her water jar, THE WOMAN WENT BACK TO THE TOWN AND SAID TO THE PEOPLE, "COME, SEE A MAN WHO TOLD ME EVERYTHING I EVER DID. Could this be the Christ?" THEY CAME OUT OF THE TOWN AND MADE THEIR WAY TOWARD HIM.

John 4:27-30 NIV

Do you wonder what made His disciples not to ask Him why He was talking to the woman even though they were surprised? It was because they knew that Jesus was delivering to the woman firsthand value added services. In fact, in the process of the conversation, Jesus told her to go and call her husband to also partake of His service value. And after she had received one of Jesus' products called "the living water", she ran out and brought more customers to Jesus through referrals. Are you treating your current customers in a way that would stimulate them to refer your products or service to others? Do you know that every customer has a network of other customers? And if you can put a smile on that customer's face with your services, you could gain a host of many others. Jesus gained a lot more prospects and they all tasted from this "living water" product. They all got personal testimonies and affirmed that what the woman told them was true. By the actions that followed, they literally said, "we have fallen in love with your products and are willing to become clients of your business brand".

Many of the Samaritans from that town believed in him because of the woman's testimony, "He told me everything I ever did." So when the Samaritans came to him, they urged him to stay with them, and he stayed two days. AND BECAUSE OF HIS WORDS MANY MORE BECAME BELIEVERS. THEY SAID TO THE WOMAN, "WE NO LONGER BELIEVE JUST BECAUSE OF WHAT YOU SAID; NOW WE HAVE HEARD FOR OURSELVES, AND WE KNOW THAT THIS MAN REALLY IS THE SAVIOR OF THE WORLD."
John 4:39-42 NIV

Did you notice that when those people came, they did not want Jesus to leave their town? They told Him to stay with them and they patronized Him for two additional days. This is marvelous! In one day Jesus expanded His kingdom business by just one good product-service delivery to one prospect. Apparently, the woman had a very robust network and Jesus was able to leverage on her network by ensuring that she was fully impacted by His product and service. Never underestimate the value of one good customer. You can expand your business into a global brand just like Jesus did by the principle of generating referrals. ***I pray that you would expand and spread your personal brand and business brand as you leverage on this principle in Jesus name!***

- **Acknowledge and commend people in your network**

Paul built a solid ministry by reason of his vast network of people across different regions, cities and nations. Without this vast network, Paul's business of sending the brand message of the gospel to the Gentiles would not have gone as far and as fast as it did. He also knew how to strengthen his networks by always commending, affirming, acknowledging and appreciating everyone in his network. Without the power of networks, Paul's ministry would have not spread so wide and so fast the way it did. Paul knew this and he always commended the key people in his network.

I commend to you our sister Phoebe, a servant of the church in Cenchrea. I ask you to receive her in the Lord in a way worthy of the saints and to give her any help she may need from you, for she has been a great help to many people, including me. Greet Priscilla and Aquila, my fellow workers in Christ Jesus. They risked their lives for me. Not only I but all the churches of the Gentiles are grateful to them. Greet also the church that meets at their house. Greet my dear friend Epenetus, who was the first convert to Christ in the province of Asia. Greet Mary, who worked very hard for you. Greet Andronicus and Junias, my relatives who have been in prison with me. They are outstanding among the apostles, and they were in Christ before I was. Greet Ampliatus, whom I love in the Lord. Greet Urbanus, our fellow worker in Christ, and my dear friend Stachys. Greet Apelles, tested and approved in Christ. Greet those who belong to the household of Aristobulus. Greet Herodion, my relative. Greet those in the household of Narcissus who are in the Lord. Greet Tryphena and Tryphosa, those women who work hard in the Lord. Greet my dear friend Persis, another woman who has worked very hard in the Lord. Greet Rufus, chosen in the Lord, and his mother, who has been a mother to me, too. Greet Asyncritus, Phlegon, Hermes, Patrobas, Hermas and the brothers with them. Greet Philologus, Julia, Nereus and his sister, and Olympas and all the saints with them.

Rom 16:1-15 NIV

Learn to always commend and affirm your appreciation to people in your network. Never take them for granted no mater who they are.

Keys for Converting the Currency of a Good Network into Tangible Wealth

- **Build healthy and viable relationships.**

In business, relationships are very vital. Relationship is critical to building a good network. And without a good network, the spread of any global business would either be limited or stagnated. People prefer to do business with those who are known to them and people would be more prone to be of help to spread your business when they like you. Focus on building relationships with people who share similar goals and visions with you. Also relate with people who have what it takes to inspire you and stir you up towards more productivity and effectiveness.

▪ Collaborate with strong partners

Most of the greatest business brands in the world today were products of solid collaborations. They came as a result of people who came together and harnessed their unique strengths for the common good of all the involved partners. Their results are always far greater than it would have been if they had worked without each other. Because they networked and worked toward a common goal, they produced astounding results. No wonder the Bible tells us that two people are better than one when there is partnership and collaboration involved. It says:

TWO CAN ACCOMPLISH MORE THAN TWICE AS MUCH AS ONE, FOR THE RESULTS CAN BE MUCH BETTER. If one falls, the other pulls him up; but if a man falls when he is alone, he's in trouble. And one standing alone can be attacked and defeated, but two can stand back-to-back and conquer; THREE IS EVEN BETTER, FOR A TRIPLE-BRAIDED CORD IS NOT EASILY BROKEN.

Eccl 4:9-10, 12 TLB

Microsoft came about as a result of the collaborative efforts of Bill Gates and his partner, Paul Allen. The greatest social media platform on earth at the moment which at this writing, boasts of about 2 billion active users globally is Facebook. It sprung up due to the collaborative efforts of Mark Zukerberg and four of his roommates at Harvard College. Apple Company is currently the largest tech company in the world and it was co-founded by Steve Jobs and Steve Wozniak. Google, the best global website in the world at this writing was co-founded by two PhD students at Stanford University during a research project. The examples are numerous, showing how that through collaborations we can tap into the power of agreement and accomplish greater feats.

Before collaborating, we must be very careful in our choice of partners in order to avoid crises and confusion in the long haul. We must also be very clear on what each party has to bring to the table in order to foster proper synergy and to ensure thorough involvement from all parties. Be very sensitive to the Holy Spirit as you build networks, partnerships and collaborations. You shall succeed as you take advantage of the currency of a good network in Jesus name!

- **Carefully select people with different complementary networks**

Jesus Christ built a global brand with this same principle of building people networks. He knew the value of raising people from different spheres of society and bringing them into alignment with his vision and purpose. He used the power of networks to build a solid influence during his days on earth and in the world today. If you study the way Jesus selected His disciples you would understand that Jesus the King from heaven is a master strategist. Jesus was very meticulous in the way He selected His disciples. He selected men with complimentary networks from different strata of the society. Jesus had such a coordinated crew with their different vast networks. No wonder His doctrine penetrated all strata of society when He walked the surface of the earth.

These are the names of the twelve apostles: first, Simon (who is called Peter) and his brother Andrew; James son of

Zebedee, and his brother John; Philip and Bartholomew; Thomas and Matthew the tax collector; James son of Alphaeus, and Thaddaeus; Simon the Zealot and Judas Iscariot, who betrayed him.

Matt 10:2-4 NIV

Observe the complementary network and strengths of Jesus' disciples. Luke was a medical doctor, Simon Peter was a professional businessman in the fishing trade. Simon also had a knack for leadership and was a go getter. Andrew was one known to have persuasion skills and networking skills, he brought his brother into the team. James and John, sons of Zebedee were also men with influence in the fishing trade. Philip was a lover of horses and had a network of people with horses and donkeys. I am sure his passion for horses and donkeys added value to the team when they were sent to get a donkey for the triumphant entry (Mark 11:1-3). There was also Matthew who had a large network of tax collectors of public revenue because he was one of them. There was a politically inclined one among His disciples known as Simon the Zealot. Zealots were a set of people who were activists and were part of a group who advocated the overthrow of the Roman rule and always stood against the efforts of the Romans to convert the Jews. These disciples of Jesus made up a very vast network because of their diverse fields and professions. Through them, Jesus was able to reach a vast network of different people more easily. Take a cue from that and select people with varying network regimes with whom you can collaborate.

- **Grow people**

There is a Chinese proverb that says "If you want 1 year of prosperity, grow grain. If you want 10 years of prosperity, grow trees. If you want 100 years of prosperity, grow people."

Sometimes the most sustaining way to ensure a good network is by investing in people development. When you build the lives of people and help them gain their grounds in life, the chances are that when such people succeed, they would not forget you. They would willingly support your vision with everything they have. They would form a solid aspect of your network and would help spread the network faster than someone who had no ties with you when he was a "nobody". Jesus Christ built the biggest establishment on earth today known as the church by virtue of His investment in people everywhere He went. He started from His twelve disciples. We can develop a powerful network of support by first providing support and value to others in their area of need. When you invest in growing people, you would be amazed how that would speak for you as you progress in life.

CHARGE
Begin to take advantage of the people network that God has blessed you with. Never take the people around you for granted because they are blessings in disguise. God would not come down physically to help you. Therefore He helps you through men whom He has raised up for your sake. He uses these men by the Holy Spirit who is the Helper. This is not to say you should look unto people. Nobody would offer you the God kind of help except the Holy Ghost urges them to. Even when He does, those people may not yield to Him. So never take it personally when people in your network do not do what is expected of them. Just remain open minded, excellent, vision focused and diligent. And when it matters most, the people you need will align to your frequency and provide what God has ordained for you through them.

AFFIRMATIONS

Thank you Father because I have a growing network that would help me make the most of my life, career and business. I am meeting the right people because I am always at the right place at the right time. I have the favour of God connecting me with the key and relevant people in my industry. I am a high value asset to everyone who comes in contact with me because I have the greater one working in me. The Holy Ghost is my help and He is perfecting all that concerns me. He has positioned men everywhere I go to partner with my vision and to help expand my business and career network. Lord I bless you!

FOOD FOR THOUGHTS

- God arranged for man to always function in a networking environment in order to achieve greater results with less effort.

- Networking is not about just connecting people. It's about connecting people with people, people with ideas, and people with opportunities.

- Building a good network is an investment in your business

- You never know a man's worth until you really know who is in his network.

- Focus on building relationships with people who share similar goals and visions with you.

NOTES

INTRODUCTION

1. Businessperson Wikipedia, the free encyclopedia, https://en.wikipedia.org/wiki/Businessperson, accessed 15/11/2017.

2. Four Million Nigerians have lost their jobs this year – NBS, Punch Newspaper, December 23, 2017, https://punchng.com/four-million-nigerians-have-lost-their-jobs-this-year-nbs/, accessed 26/12/2017.

CHAPTER ONE

1. Order of the British Empire - Wikipedia, the free encyclopedia, https://en.wikipedia.org/wiki/Order_of_the_British_Empire, accessed 16/11/2017.

2. I never allowed autism to stop me from achieving greatness – Imafidon, Oxford Don, Punch Newspaper, Nov 18, 2017, http://punchng.com/i-never-allowed-autism-stigma-stop-me-from-achieving-greatness-imafidon-oxford-don/, accessed 25/11/2017.

CHAPTER TWO

1. Napoleon Hill, "Think and Grow Rich", (London: Vermilion, 2004), pg 24.

2. History of Apple Inc. Wikipedia, the free encyclopedia, https://en.wikipedia.org/wiki/History_of_Apple_Inc, accessed 20/11/2017.

3. Steve Jobs: An Extraordinary Career, https://www.entrepreneur.com/article/197538, accessed 20/11/2017.

4. Dr. Myles Munroe, "The Principles and Power of Vision", (Pennsylvania: Whittaker House, 2003), pg 35.

5. Jacquelyn Smith, "7 things you probably didn't know about your job search" – Forbes, April 13, 2013, https://www.forbes.com/sites/jacquelynsmith/2013/04/17/7-things-you-probably-didnt-know-about-your-job-search/#32abb72c3811, accessed 22/11/2017.

6. List of Nikola Tesla Patents – Wikipedia, the free encyclopedia, https://en.wikipedia.org/wiki/List_of_Nikola_Tesla_patents, accessed 23/11/2017.

7. Nikola Tesla - Wikipedia, the free encyclopedia, https://en.wikipedia.org/wiki/Nikola_Tesla, accessed 23/11/2017.

8. FULL TRANSCRIPT: President Obama's speech on the 50th anniversary of the March on Washington, Washington Post, August 28, 2013, https://www.washingtonpost.com/politics/transcript-president-obamas-speech-on-the-50th-anniversary-of-the-march-on-washington/2013/08/28/0138e01e-0ffb-11e3-8cdd-bcdc09410972_story.html?utm_term=.715c6af72f9

2, accessed 24/11/2017.

9. Dr. Myles Munroe, "The Principles and Power of Vision", (Pennsylvania: Whittaker House, 2003), pg 17-18.

CHAPTER THREE
1. Hard Currency – Investopedia, https://www.investopedia.com/terms/h/hardcurrency.asp, accessed 26/11/2017.

2. Benjamin Franklin – Wikipedia, the free encyclopedia, https://en.wikipedia.org/wiki/Benjamin_Franklin, accessed 25/11/2017.

3. The autobiography of Benjamin Franklin – USHistory.org, http://www.ushistory.org/franklin/autobiography/page37.htm, accessed 25/11/2017.

4. Ronke Sanya, "How I Got 'Greatest Surprise Gift' From Typist – Osinbajo", November 15, 2017, Channels TV, https://www.channelstv.com/2017/11/15/how-i-got-greatest-surprise-gift-from-typist-osinbajo/, accessed 24/11/2017.

5. Mohamed Jalloh, "Jack Ma: Success Story", https://www.investopedia.com/university/jack-ma-biography/jack-ma-success-story.asp, accessed 28/11/2017.

6. Aliko Dangote – Wikipedia, the free encyclopedia,

https://en.wikipedia.org/wiki/Aliko_Dangote, accessed 27/11/2017.

7. Udeme Akpan, "The promise of Dangote's $12bn refinery – Vanguard News", August 27, 2017, https://www.vanguardngr.com/2017/08/promise-dangotes-12bn-refinery/, accessed 27/11/2017.

8. Brian Tracy, "Goals", (California : Berrett-Koehler, 2002), pg 246-249.

9. Thomas Alva Edison, http://alg.umbc.edu/rogers/edison/edison.htm, accessed 30/11/2017.

CHAPTER FOUR
1. Alfred Nobel – Wikipedia, the free encyclopedia, https://en.wikipedia.org/wiki/Alfred_Nobel, accessed 2/12/2017.

2. Benjamin Franklin – Wikipedia, the free encyclopedia, https://en.wikipedia.org/wiki/Benjamin_Franklin, accessed 2/12/2017.

3. George Washington's Rules of Civility and Decent Behavior in company and conversation, http://www.foundationsmag.com/civility.html, accessed 3/12/2017.

ABOUT THE AUTHOR

Iredafenevesho Owolabi is a seasoned teacher and preacher of the message of the Kingdom of God. He is happily married to Pharm. Dr. Precious Owolabi, the love of his life and together they are affecting lives for the Kingdom. He is a graduate of Chemical Engineering Department, University of Benin and a professional Software Developer. The literal meaning of his first name is "the kingdom of God has come into my house". That is why he is popularly called "the Kingdom Man".

He is a prolific author of several books. He speaks at events and platforms on several topics ranging from Creativity, Authorpreneurship, 4D-Thinking, Entrepreneurship, Problem Solving, Leadership, Unlocking your potential, Kingdom and so on.

www.ingramcontent.com/pod-product-compliance
Lightning Source LLC
Chambersburg PA
CBHW052151220526
45471CB00004B/1628